come back, judy baba

come back, judy baba

Memoirs of India

Mary Hargreaves Norbury
& Judy Norbury

For my new friend, Amy,
Happy travels!
Love Judy

Madrona Books & Publishing

Published by
Madrona Books & Publishing
3909 Marine Drive
Royston, BC V0R 2V0

Editors: Barbara Pulling and Margaret Cadwaladr
Book Design: John McKercher

LIBRARY AND ARCHIVES CANADA CATALOGUING IN PUBLICATION

Norbury, Mary Hargreaves, 1922–
Come back, Judy Baba : memoirs of India / by Mary Hargreaves Norbury and Judy Norbury.

ISBN 978-0-9730096-5-1

1. Norbury, Mary Hargreaves, 1922–. 2. India—Biography.
3. Norbury, Judy, 1949– —Travel. 4. India—Description and travel.
I. Norbury, Judy, 1949– II. Title.
DS481.N67N67 2008 954.04'2092 C2008-904527-0

Printed in Canada on recycled paper by Transcontinental

contents

Part Two: Judy's Story

introduction

In the fall and winter of 1996-97, I returned to India, the land of my birth. This book is a result of that journey. I was thrilled to be going back. Accompanied by my partner Ross and my twelve-year-old daughter Belinda, I traversed the sub-continent.

My parents' story of India is a true fairytale romance. My mother, Mary Hargreaves, was one of Vancouver's top models, and during the 1940s she worked at an exclusive ladies clothing shop in downtown Vancouver. My father, Mike Norbury, had left his home in England in 1930 at the age of eighteen to work at an Indian carpet-manufacturing company, one of many that had operated along the Ganges River between Allahabad and Varanasi since the reign of Akbar the Great. At the end of Second World War, after six years as a major in the Indian army, he spent some months studying photography in New York. Then he settled in Vancouver for a time.

My father was walking along Howe Street early one morning. Reflected in a shop window, he saw a tall elegant woman with a blond streak in her swept-up hair and a gold belt around her waist. He stared at what he called "this beautiful apparition." By the time he'd turned to look her in person, she had disappeared. But they were destined to meet. Later that week he was working on a photographic essay of Stanley Park for National Geographic. He asked a friend if he knew any models that might be willing to come to Stanley Park for a photo shoot. This friend gave him the address of a dress shop on Howe Street and told him to ask for Mary. The woman who came out from the back of the shop in response to his query, was the lovely woman he'd seen reflected in the window.

At the time, my mother was semi-engaged to another man. This didn't stop my father from becoming a family friend of Mary's parents—Gladys and Will Hargreaves. He was often invited to the house for weekend dinners and joined the family for Christmas and New Year celebrations. My mother's previous engagement just faded away.

It was 1947. India gained independence from Britain on August 15, and parts of the country were in great turmoil. But early in January 1948, my father received word that the carpet company wanted him to return to become a director of the firm.

On January 27th 1948, my mother and father spent their first evening alone together at the Cave Supper Club. Mary was very surprised and upset to learn that Mike was leaving for India in the morning.

My father returned to Mirzapur. Finding things to be as peaceful as they had been in 1930, he proposed to my mother by letter. She accepted and boarded a freighter bound for Bombay. After a long sea voyage, my mother married my father on September 11, 1948 in the Bombay Cathedral. Afterwards, they travelled by train to a spacious company bungalow on the banks of the Ganges River near the city of Mirzapur. Ten months later, I was born in the hill station of Mussoorie. Four years after my birth, I became ill with polio in this same town. My mother flew back to Canada with my sister and me as soon as I was able to travel. I spent a year in hospital, had several operations and painful therapy. I also began to use a wheelchair for mobility.

During the first couple of years following our family's settling in Vancouver, my mother began work on an account of her life as a post-Raj Memsahib. My sisters and I were always aware that the 'book' existed and that publishers had turned down her memoir due to the tragic ending of her tale. A friend had typed out my mother's manuscript and made copies for members of our family. Shortly before leaving for India, I read her entire story for the first time. The account provides a fascinating glimpse of a life of luxury and privilege as seen through the eyes of a Canadian girl who came of age during the depression. I was able to see my mother in a new and more sympathetic light. Ours had been a sometimes-stormy relationship.

Following my return from India, I began to work on a manuscript of my own. Realizing that my story is the real ending to my mother's story, I combined them into one continuous tale. My parents displayed the colonial attitudes of their time in India, but I decided to honour my mother's text as it was written. Her writings are reproduced with only small changes here and there, mostly for clarity.

Writing this has allowed me to understand the circumstances that made her who she is and how that has shaped me. Her experiences in India and my return to India complete the story.

Judy Norbury
Vancouver Island, BC
2008

Amritsar
Mussorie
Dehra Dun
Delhi
New Delhi
Bikaner
Agra
Jaipur
Pushkar
Kanpur
Allahabad
Benares
Mirzapur
INDIA
Bhopal
Jabalpur
Ahmadabad
Kolkata
(Calcutta)
Mumbai
(Bombay)
Arabian
Sea
Bay of
Bengal
Goa
Hubli
Hampi
Bangalore
Chennai
(Madras)
Mysore
Mudumalai
Ootacamund
Calicut
Alleppey
Varkala
Trivandrum
Kovalam
Kanyakumari

BOOK I

Mary's Story

1

River

The Ganges was in flood. She roared over the sand on the opposite side for as far as one could see. The tops of trees barely showed above her angry waters, and taking refuge in them were snakes, scorpions and animals, their fear of one another forgotten as they clung together, inching higher and higher as the waters rose.

Mike and I stood on the high banks, watching the swirling waters below and saying a lingering goodbye before he left for his first day's work at the office since our honeymoon. It was all rather romantic. The wind caught at my hair, unpinned it and blew it wildly about. Wind whipped up whitecaps on the monsoon-swollen river and helped send the thick black clouds that came rushing up from Calcutta on their way to Bombay.

"I'll be back for lunch" Mike said, "the office is only just up the road."

"I'll be waiting at the end of the driveway," I told him.

He kissed me and then gazed at me tenderly. "There's something I forgot to tell you."

"What is it?" I whispered.

"The body pusher," Mike answered.

"The WHAT?"

"The body pusher. If you ever notice a peculiar odour and see a lot of activity amongst the vultures, call the sweeper and say, "Dom ko balao—got it? Dom ko balao," and Suleiman will fetch the body pusher. He's an old man employed by the company to push bodies away when they become lodged along the river bank."

Kissing me once more, Mike hopped on his bike and cycled away to the office.

Body pusher. What kind of a body? Mike hadn't said. A human body? What a stir that always caused back home in Vancouver whenever a corpse was discovered in the Fraser River. Screaming sirens, reporters and headlines in the local papers. Here it seemed to be the accepted thing. I visualized an old man with a long pole (very long, I hoped) giving the corpse a disinterested shove and sending it twisting and turning on its way to the next body pusher, and so on, down a long line of old men until it reached Calcutta, 800 miles downstream.

I glanced down at my feet, thrust into sandals made of the barest scraps of leather, and wriggled my toes contentedly. For me it was the end of high heels, stockings and girdles. No more standing on my feet eight hours every workday, no more swollen ankles and—best of all—no more rushing.

Here in India, close by a small village and not far from the city of Mirzapur, I found that people seldom hurried, never fretted over a lost minute or a wasted day. The years of accelerated living slipped away as if they had never been. Indian style, I squatted on the bank as I watched the frothy, foamy whirlpools below. I thought back to the life I had so recently left, and how it had come about that I found myself in the land I had always yearned to see.

2

the suzette sportswear shop

VANCOUVER, the city of my birth, was a fast-growing city of around half a million in 1947. Except for a brief period of schooling and work in England, I had lived there all my life. Her natural harbour, with its scenic backdrop of majestic mountains, drew many thousands of people each year. Not only tourists but also prairie folk, tired of the extreme prairie weather and the flat uninteresting countryside, left their homes in Edmonton, Winnipeg and Saskatoon to flock out west. Those on holiday played tennis and golf amid the unbelievable beauty of Stanley Park, or swam at Kitsilano Beach, Spanish Banks or English Bay. Taking leisurely trips around Marine Drive and stopping to gaze at the Pacific Ocean, with Vancouver Island lying in the distance, they decided that this was it, the city of their dreams. One by one, they vowed to sell up and make Vancouver their home. The rain came as a shock to many and drove scores away, but others quickly took their place. Across the inlet in North and West Vancouver, forests were ruthlessly cleared and new homes dotted the mountainside. As the prairie folk moved in, more Vancouverites moved out. All through New Westminster, the Royal City, and over the Fraser River and beyond, new housing developments sprang up where a short time before only an occasional farm had stood. And so Vancouver grew and spread. People commuted to work each day over broad new highways, joining the endless stream of cars that poured in and out of the city. Buses and rattling old streetcars were jam packed, and it was a case of the survival of the fittest as people pushed, shoved and elbowed their way aboard.

On to these streetcars, I, too, pushed each night, weary from standing all day. With a practiced eye, I would scan the faces of those seated, seeking someone clutching a pink transfer that meant they would be leaving the car before me. My home was near the end of the line. In no time at all, I would find myself back with the same faces on my way to work in the morning.

The Suzette Sportswear Shop stood on Howe Street, an exclusive part of town close to the better hotels. We stocked English woolens, cashmere sweaters and hand made belts and jewelry. As Vancouver grew, Suzettes added lingerie, hats and dresses to the stock. Below, tailors worked over custom made suits, coats and slacks in British tweed. We were well known to the American tourists, who raved over our hand woven cloth, and English and Scottish sweaters, while office girls cheerfully went into debt to own an outfit bearing a Suzette label. We enviously outfitted customers for Honolulu, Europe and other equally exciting places. If we felt a little jealous as we packed their exciting clothes in layers of tissue, we didn't show it. Seattle or Vancouver Island was as far as we got for our holidays, and there wasn't much we could do about it.

Before paydays, when we were reduced to taking our own lunch, we sat in the little staff room trading sandwiches and discussing the favourite topic of millions of salesgirls and office workers the world over. Easing tired feet out of our shoes, we talked of the things we would buy and the places we would visit if, by some glorious chance, we suddenly came into money. We daydreamed our way by air, ship and train to every corner of the globe.

"India," I would say breathlessly. "India's my choice."

Although the others didn't share my enthusiasm for the Far East, India, for some strange reason, urgently pulled at me on invisible strings, across the 10,000 odd miles that separated us.

One afternoon as I pressed clothes for a window display, my mother, who worked with me, came to tell me I was wanted at the front of the shop.

"Who is it?" I asked.

"I don't know," Mom replied. "He's dressed in rather an odd way, and terribly English."

We peeked around the corner, and I spied a stocky man standing by the door. Under a black beret, tight curly hair grew low on his neck. He wore an old raincoat, ancient green cords, a spotted scarf and good shoes. Slung across his shoulders hung a knapsack and an expensive-looking camera. I walked up to him and found he possessed one of the most beautiful accents I had ever heard. Fascinated by his voice, I listened as he explained why he had come. He wanted models for some outdoor shots, and a photographer friend sent him to me.

"Would I help?"

I agreed, and after making arrangements to meet, he thanked me and left. No sooner had he disappeared out the door than all the girls who had been spying from behind the pillars came rushing up and demanded to know, "Whoever is he?"

"His name's Michael Norbury and he's a photographer. I've promised to meet him next Sunday with some other models and pose for him."

"What a queer way to dress!" they all chorused.

"I don't care," I replied absently. "I like him."

We met Mike early Sunday in Stanley Park—Jackie, blonde and beautiful, Ethel with the flaming red hair, Tessa, Blig, Tish and dark, shapely Lee. We all cycled around the park and stopped by Brockton Point, Lost Lagoon and the gardens while Mike posed us and took pictures.

3

Mike

FROM THE AGE OF 18, Mike had lived in India, leaving his home in Worcestershire to join a carpet-manufacturing firm in Mirzapur, United Provinces. At the beginning of the war, he joined the Indian Army, fought in the Burma campaign and at the war's end found it impossible to settle to Mirzapur's quite uneventful life. Resigning as a director of the company, Mike set off for New York to take up his hobby of photography seriously.

I was strongly attracted to this sturdy, curly-headed Englishman and we spent hours talking of all manner of things, always returning to my favourite subject—the Far East. I listened entranced while he spoke of the strange habits and customs of India. These hours, though, were always spent in the company of other people, mainly my current boyfriend. Mike's English sense of fair play, much to my annoyance, limited him to visits to my home, joining my friend and me for a drink or taking Lee and me out for coffee. Patiently waiting for signs that my romance was wilting at the edges, he one day in January threw all caution to the wind, said to hell with fair play, cricket and all that, and invited me out to dinner. We sat in a crowded nightclub oblivious to the blaring orchestra while I listened to Mike tell me that he was returning to India.

"India is a troubled country now," he explained. "Riots and fighting have been going on for months, but she is too much in my blood to stay away. I must go back."

"Soon?" I asked.

"Tomorrow morning," he answered.

I grew more miserable by the hour at the thought of his leaving. As surely as he knew he must go, I knew that I wanted him to stay. He left me at the door with no mention of the things I wanted to hear. After tucking a package in my hand, he strode off down the street and, as I thought, out of my life. I watched until he was out of sight, and then turned in the door. Flinging off my coat, I switched on the light and unwrapped his gift. Nestled in a piece of cotton wool lay a beautiful emerald and diamond pin.

Wires burned their way up from San Francisco, cables across the seas from Calcutta and then the day came when I arrived home to find a letter waiting for me postmarked "Mirzapur."

"The riots and troubles India have been experiencing haven't affected Mirzapur," Mike wrote. "It is as quiet and peaceful as ever."

Riots had been stealthily planned, but nobody ever turned up to take part in them. Mahatma Gandhi had been assassinated and now, after this great shock and tremendous loss to India, the country was gradually settling down. No longer had Mike any fear of asking me out to be his wife. Would I join him the following September, when the hot weather would be at an end and the rains well started? We would be married in Bombay, and I could choose Kashmir, Ceylon or Darjeeling for our honeymoon. I reread this exciting proposal.

"Listen to this, Mom," I called, and I read it to her.

"Hasn't he got a nerve?" I exclaimed. "He asks me to marry him on one page, and on the next he tells me the best time to go out."

"He's certainly sure of himself," my mother remarked.

"He sure is," I agreed. Then I rushed to the phone to call Lee and tell her that I would be leaving for India in the summer.

4

Preparations

CARTONS OF SPRING and summer clothes were opened and checked off in the overcrowded stock room at Suzette's. Many a cotton dress was whipped away before it ever saw the front of the shop and hung on a rack labeled with my name. I suffered pangs of guilt when a customer enquired after a certain outfit she had seen in Mademoiselle or Vogue magazine.

"I've looked through every rack, but you don't seem to have it," she would say sadly.

"Sorry," I would murmur sympathetically.

We had it, alright—hanging in the back hidden under a dust sheet with 'Miss Hargreaves' pinned upon it. But it was my turn now.

Lee and I often crouched down behind a counter and whispered excitedly.

"Show me the house again, Mary," she would exhort. I would take out the worn envelope of photos Mike had sent, and together we'd examine them.

"Bungalow," he calls it. Look at the size of it. Just think, Mary, you're going to live there!"

We would talk and giggle on until interrupted by the irate face of a customer peering down at us.

Many customers became good friends, but as in all stores, there were the few types we dreaded to see approach the door. On these occasions there silently took place a grand exodus of the older girls. We disappeared behind counters, or into fitting rooms or locked ourselves in the john and left customers to the extra help, or new girls. We knew them all: the ones who never bought anything, the shoplifters and spotters from

The bungalow at Mirzapur.

other stores. I had longed often to step out of the polite salesgirl role and tell them off, but as the time grew nearer for me to leave, I found they no longer irritated me. Instead, I pitied them.

"In only a few short months I shall be on my way," I told myself, my tummy doing flip-flops at the thought of over a month at sea and trunks filled with exciting clothes. "These people will still be coming in, nothing will have changed, while I shall be visiting strange ports on my way to marry the nicest man in the world."

"I shall learn the language," I confided to Ethel. What a wonderful surprise it would be for Mike when I stepped from the car at the door of the bungalow, gave a graceful salaam as I had seen them do in the movies, and then commenced to chatter away to the servants in fluent Hindustani. I could see them all staring in open-mouthed amazement and Mike, with an astonished look on his face, gazing at me proudly. I had over six months in which to learn.

"Plenty of time," Ethel agreed, so we went to a bookshop on Granville Street one day during our lunch hour and bought "Hugo's Hindustani Simplified." Each evening I sat on the crowded streetcar with my nose buried in the little book, muttering to myself. "Ghora" was a horse and "Gora" a white man. I should have to be careful there, I could see. "Apke bhaike pas ek ghora hai"—"Your brother's possession a horse it." "They ready not are, we glad not are." Weeks later I was still getting a white man mixed up with a horse, and I came to the dreary conclusion that it didn't seem simplified enough for me. The book gathered dust as I began learning how to sew. Mom hired a machine and I practiced each evening, but instead of lifting my foot from the pedal when I wanted to stop, I had an odd nervous reaction and pressed harder. "I'll master this thing if it kills me," I told myself grimly as I sewed crooked seams up the sides of a pair of silk panties. After the threads were tied and the pants ready for pressing, Mom discovered that I had sewn the legs up completely. Back went the machine, but not before Mom had run up a cool wedding dress in white Swiss islet.

This was the year of the new long look in clothes. Short skirts had been worn for so many years that the sudden descent of the hemline came as a great shock. Women discussed it, magazines hinted at it, but Suzette's had it, and what an odd feeling it was as the hems of our skirts swirled about our ankles in an unfamiliar way. Long plaid skirts swung gracefully to and fro, worn with white long-sleeved Gibson girl blouses and flat shoes. Coats with yards of material in the back and detachable hoods were worn slung over our shoulders. Suit skirts were long and slim, so that we walked with a jerky motion and often split them right up to our knees as we climbed the high steps of the streetcars.

Gold bags with belts and sandals to match were worn with cotton dresses.

With the austerity of the war years behind them, designers went wild with colours and materials. It was a perfect year to plan a trousseau. The shipping office confirmed my passage on a Norwegian freighter, the "Silver Spray". She carried 12 passengers, sailed from San Francisco on July 29th and would be calling in at Manilla, Singapore and Colombo before reaching Bombay in September.

Climbing aboard the streetcar the morning the last day at work, I slid into my seat and gazed around at my fellow passengers. It was a funny thing, I always thought. With the exception of those who worked together, people who travelled to work daily on the same buses and streetcars never seemed to speak to one another. You seldom found out where they worked, nor did you care, but you knew their wardrobe intimately and noted each new purchase with interest. Their hairstyle, jewellery and accessories were familiar to you, also their taste in reading matter, but the people themselves were only recognizable on your streetcar at 8:10 AM or 5:45 at night. Should you see them on Granville Street, you would pass them by with the fleeting thought that there goes someone you should know. Near me sat a woman I had long ago labelled as a "Mrs. MacNatcher." I had watched her all through the war years as she knitted countless miles for the Red Cross. She had lately turned to diamond socks, and as I studied her latest colour scheme, I wondered how she managed to keep all the tiny balls of wool from tangling. The girl who got off a block past Woodward's had on a new blouse. Style No. 481 by Joseph, price $8.95, I automatically noted to myself. Down at the far end of the car sat a prim-looking man who read rude magazines hidden behind the morning newspaper.

"Tomorrow morning," I thought, "just as if a whole day and night hadn't passed by, this car will be the same, only I shan't be here. As I hear it rumble down the tracks a short block from home, I shall simply turn over and snuggle deeper down in bed. It's my last day!" I wanted to shout at them. Just think, my last day.

5

Moonlight on the Ganges

THE "SILVER SPRAY" looked just like her name—beautiful. She was tied up amongst the rusty old freighters in San Francisco harbour, and I was proud to be sailing on her. The tearful parting from my family was behind me, and as I climbed the gangplank, I felt at last I was well and truly on my way.

My large, tastefully furnished cabin was off the deck reserved for passengers, and the adjoining bathroom I shared with a tall, slender girl from California. Dorothy Marshall—not yet 19—belonged to the Scandinavian Mission, and after studying the language in Mussoorie, a hill station in northern India, she would travel on up to the borders of Nepal and Tibet to teach. Dorothy and I spent most of our time with Charles Matsch, a short, good-looking Texan who was travelling out to Afghanistan, also to teach.

As the weather grew warmer and the coast of California fell behind us, Axel, the first officer rapped smartly on our doors at 6 AM, telling us it was time for our morning dip in the pool the crew had rigged up on deck. It was fascinating yet frightening to pull us up by the side of the pool and look over at the Pacific racing by only a few feet below. Coming out of the water, we wrapped ourselves in huge towels and shared steaming mugs of thick creamy coffee with Axel. While the sun grew hotter each moment, we lay back idly smoking and waiting for the time to shower and dress for breakfast. Eighteen days later, we reached Manila. We were tanned to a deep brown, our hair bleached by the sun and

Mary and Mike's wedding in Bombay.

seawater. Our appetites had increased to such an extent that waiting for the gong to ring for meals became sheer torture.

For almost a week in Singapore, we left the ship each day to explore and be shown the city by the ship's officers and Eva, the "Silver Spray" wireless operator. We danced and drank in the Raffles Hotel and poked about in the very heart of that attractive, sprawling city. So it was all really true: the East was as fascinating as I had always imagined it to be. Through my gradual introduction to it, well could I understand how it crept into one's blood and stayed there, never allowing those fortunate to have tasted its pleasures ever again to be completely happy elsewhere. We danced out under the stars at the Airport Hotel. The moon never looked so fat nor the stars so close, nor the soft breeze that ruffled my hair so warm and inviting.

"Roll on, Bombay," I thought. If ever there was a climate to start married life in, this was it! Colombo with its incredibly white sandy beaches, the Galle Face Hotel, rickshaw rides in the moonlight and hibiscus blossom in my hair, and then we were ploughing our way to Bombay and I received a wire: "Welcome to Hindustan, darling."

We anchored in the bay. Dorothy, Charlie and I leaned on the rail and watched the city, which lay under a low haze. In the third boat that came out to us, I spotted Mike, half hidden behind a huge bouquet of flowers. The excitement of our meeting over, we sat in a quiet corner of the lounge, and Mike slipped a ring of aquamarine and diamonds on my finger. Two days later, we were married in the Cathedral. After a reception in the Taj Mahal Hotel and a few days of shopping and sightseeing, we packed and left for Mirzapur.

On our way to the station, we drove down Grant Road, where hundreds of thousands of refugees from Pakistan were living, huddled together. They overflowed onto the platform of the station, and we stepped gingerly over their bodies. "Salaam Memsahib, baksheesh Memsahib, Gari Purva Memsahib," and they stretched out their claw-like hands and clutched at my skirt.

"What are they saying, Mike?" I asked as I stared in horror at the scene around us.

"They are asking you for money and calling you Protector of the Poor."

"Oh, how awful, can't we give them something?"

"Nothing, I'm afraid. Look at them. There are thousands. Give to one and you would be surrounded in no time."

Starvation showed in their gaunt faces and their staring eyes. It showed in the distended stomachs of the little children running about on thin bowed legs. Seeing my face, Mike gently said, "I'm sorry, darling, I had forgotten how you feel when first you see it, but believe me you get used to it, and learn to ignore it. One has to or one couldn't stay. There's nothing we can do for these poor wretches here, but there is lots we can do to help our servants and the weavers at home, you'll see."

I stood close to him while he carried on a rapid conversation with the conductor. He was frowning. "What is it, Mike?" I asked.

"The air-conditioned train has broken down, and we shall have to go by ordinary coach."

"That's alright, isn't it?" I asked.

"But we haven't any bedding rolls, and only one pillow," Mike explained.

"Bedding rolls? Do you have to take your own bedding?"

"Yes, of course, unless you go by air-conditioned as I had planned, then it's supplied." Mike whispered a few words to Bagoti, the office clerk who was staying to see to my heavy luggage, and Bagoti dashed off.

"In here, Mary, we shall just have to make do." Mike helped me up into our compartment. It had two long leather seats, electric fans overhead and off to one side a tiny bathroom complete with shower. We settled down, and had a brandy. As the train slid out of the station, Bagoti came flying down the platform waving a roll of toilet paper!

Throughout the journey, I sat with my nose pressed flat against the window, watching the countryside flash by. At every station, we got out to stretch our legs and mingle with the crowds while I plagued Mike with questions. There was always something to hold your interest; things to set you laughing and scenes to make you cry. Wild-eyed holy men, their hair matted and tangled, their nearly naked bodies covered with the fine grey ash of cow dung. Beautiful doe-eyed women gracefully weaving in and out of the crowds as they followed a few paces behind their husbands. Adorable children with firm little fat brown bottoms. Through the throngs of people, the station coolies in their bright red turbans, piled high with luggage, jog-trotted along the platform. The spicy smell of curry, the sweetmeat man and the ice cream man, their cries mingling with the "Gharam pani" call of the water carrier. Strange exciting sounds, strange exotic smells. Some pleasant, many unpleasant, I thought, screwing up my nose as I watched people squatting by the tracks to answer nature's call. It's simple, really, I thought; no mad rushing off to hotels if you missed your train. You simply camped on the platform and lived there until the next one came along. Groups of people were busily preparing meals. Mothers sat calmly feeding their babies, and those who grew weary curled up in a ball and fell asleep.

Night came. I produced two sheets, a belated wedding gift. Mike gave me the pillow and we went to bed. The train roared on through the darkness. At various stops we were interrupted by heavy pounding on the doors as people called to be let in. Some whispered softly, "Memsahib, Memsahib," but quickly vanished when Mike roared, "Go to hell!"

"It's no longer safe for women to travel alone in India," Mike told me. "A woman may unwittingly open the door instead of staying put, leaving herself wide open to robbery or even murder. It occurs very seldom, really, but as in other countries, it does happen. This time tomorrow night we'll be home," Mike went on. "The servants are beside themselves with excitement over your coming and have been bossing me about in the most extraordinary way. The Memsahib must have this, the

Memsahib must have that. Good night, Memsahib, darling." And with a sigh, Mike promptly fell asleep amidst the din and shouting of a station we had just pulled into, while I battled with the endless streams of large brown cockroaches that marched out of the bathroom and over me.

"Moonlight on the Ganges is a sight you'll never forget," Mike had written to tell me before I left home. "There will be a full moon on the night we arrive in Mirzapur, and I can't wait for you to see it."

I had dreamed over and over of my arrival at the station, the drive through the city and my first glimpse of the bungalow. Mike and I, hand in hand, would walk up and down the lawn, watching the moon on the river. As it turned out, the short trip from the station to the house was the most difficult part of the whole journey. Rain! Sheets and sheets of the most terrific rain poured down, and visibility was nil. Long forms under massive black umbrellas leapt up and down the platform yelling orders, tripping over one another and mislaying our bags. One figure in white paddled out of the darkness and held an umbrella high above me, then salaamed.

"Go with Hamid, Mary, he'll see you to the car," Mike shouted. I gestured for Hamid to share the umbrella, but flashing huge teeth at me, he refused.

Dodging rearing ekka ponies and splashing through lakes of water, we reached the Morris and I was handed in, while a station wagon was loaded with our luggage. We drove off, the night pitch black and the road before us like a river. The car plunged through the water, then coughed, spluttered, and died. Mike struggled with it but it refused to budge. Opening the window, he yelled back for the station wagon to drive up and take us on. They did, but so close to our door that there was no room to open it. "There's a ditch on my side, move away, move away!" Mike hollered, then let loose a flood of Hindustani. Finally, with much grinding of gears and racing of the engine, it was all sorted out, and we continued on our way in the station wagon.

The lights of the bungalow glowed faintly through the rain as we turned in the driveway. Mike lifted me out of the car and carried me into the house. His hair was plastered to his head. His shirt, wringing wet from perspiration and rain, clung to him, and his glasses were covered with little droplets of water. He dropped me rather unromantically into a chair and I started to giggle. Moonlight on the Ganges! Never mind—there would be lots of moons for me to watch in the years to come. Right now, we were isolated on a cosy island of our own here in the drawing room. A bottle of iced champagne lay ready to open, with a plate of hot samosas nearby. Fans whirled lazily overhead. Outside the rain continued in a thunderous roar.

6

Bisundapur Bungalow

So, at long last, I was really here. Now I was standing on the banks of the Ganges, faced with the thought that it was quite in order to find singed corpses lying about at the foot of our garden. The river had washed whole villages away, leaving thousands homeless, covering their pitiful pieces of land and destroying carpet looms, taking away their very living and leaving these wretched people with nothing but their unshakable faith in the holy Mother Ganges. Our firm would supply bricks for new houses and replace looms, but what of the others not employed by us? What, I wondered, happened to them?

It was hot and humid, and my clothes clung limply to me. As the heavens opened up and released another deluge, I hurried into the bungalow to start my day. The house had been completely painted inside before my arrival, but Mike had left the arranging to me. Half-naked men swarmed through the rooms, painters, carpenters and electricians, while outside on the veranda Guafur, the dirzi or tailor, sat cross-legged on the floor by his little hand machine, turning out neatly sewn covers for chesterfields and chairs. Everything about Guafur appeared to be held together by rusty old pieces of wire. Not only the vintage sewing machines, and his scissors—even his spectacles, perched halfway down his nose, were wired to his ears. By pantomime and with a few English words like "frills" and "tucks" thrown in, I showed Guafur what I wanted done, thankful that he would never discover that my one and only attempt at needlework had turned out a failure.

The men climbed rickety bamboo ladders, each rung secured with string and old rags. I had loved the old cream bungalow on sight and, deciding against a honeymoon away, settled down to the exciting job of arranging the spacious rooms and letting my imagination run wild.

I turned first to the drawing room. Thirty by fourteen feet, it had a fireplace at one end. Ten glass doors opposite opened out onto a broad veranda facing the riverbank. Huge electric fans hung from the 18-foot high ceiling, and the walls, woodwork and floor were painted cream. The house was full of dark heavy furniture left behind by the various Sahibs and Memsahibs through the years, and the first thing I wanted done was to lower the height of the tables and chairs. This request was met by stares of astonishment and disapproval as I indicated what I wanted by wild sawing motions. This Memsahib was mad, completely mad.

"Cut the legs down on this beautiful table? Paint it cream?" the painters asked. Shaking their heads in a bewildered fashion, they carried out the orders, but I could tell by their expression that if these things had suited other Sahibs and Memsahibs fifty years ago, why not me? A long, low coffee table was constructed using some curved legs off an old fire stool and an ancient wardrobe door. Fat clay water pots from the bazaar were turned into lamps, and Guafur made shades out of heavy cream silk. We ordered yards of bright chintz from Bombay, and he made covers for the nicely shaped chesterfield, two chairs, a footstool, and a large low lounge. The extra chairs were covered in bright yellow hand woven cloth. Upon the cream floor, we laid a grass-green carpet, leaving enough space around the edge for five differently shaped scatter rugs of a cream background, centered with coloured flowers and edged with thick fluffy wool fringes. These were gifts to me from Mike, but the one I prized above all others was the nine-foot circular carpet on the center of the green rug.

The dining room, identical in shape and size, was next. Here the glass doors opened onto the front veranda, which faced the driveway and the road that wound by our bungalow and on through the little village of Bisundapur. The floor of the dining room was painted pale grey, and upon it lay a beautiful Indian rug in an ancient Persian design, coloured with rich reds, wines and royal blue.

A wedding gift of Chinese tapestry in blues and wine was made into a screen that stood in front of the fireplace during the hot weather. The carpenters attacked an ugly black sideboard. They removed its legs and grotesque sidepieces, and it ended up painted grey to match the floor. The drapes covering one entire end of the room and those by each door were wine. Off to one side of the dining room stood the den. Here, with the walls and woodwork ivory, I left the furniture in its original dark wood. Two high winged chairs were covered in loosely woven cream cloth to match the lounge, and the "tree of life" curtains that hung by the doors blended with the deep pile carpet. There remained the guest rooms, dressing rooms and our bedroom to be done, but the main part of the house was finished.

Previously skeptical about all this chopping and changing, the servants now viewed each room with pride, announcing to my delight that there wasn't a nicer bungalow in all Hindustan. But I knew that most of them had never been out of Mirzapur and that ours was probably one of the few European houses they had ever been in.

Five of the bungalow's seventeen rooms were bathrooms. Mine, off from my dressing room, was large and square. The stone floor was painted red and the walls were whitewashed. The tub was a proper English one; there were only two of them in the house, the other being in a guest room. Mike preferred the oval tin tub, where he could sink away down and pretend he was in the cockpit of a plane. Every time he bathed, he shot down innumerable enemy aircraft while the tub rocked to and fro and the water sloshed over the floor to disappear down the drains and end up watering the rose garden outside our bedroom door. Leaping out of the tub, he would grab a gurrah, (clay pot used to keep water cool), dump the icy water over him and then fling the gurrah to the other side of the room, where it smashed into a thousand pieces. "They only cost a few annas," he explained. "It's good for the potteries business, and what's more, keeps me from getting ulcers!"

A low wall enclosing my tub was where my gurrahs rested. As they were favourite places for snakes to coil about, and Mike knew my horror of snakes, he had sliding trap doors set over the drain. They were never closed, though, and eventually they rusted up well over the opening, so that in the beginning I always took a bath with one eye on the drain, expecting at any moment to see a cobra emerge from the garden. What I would do in that event took up hours of thought, but in the end, I felt sure that I should, without the slightest hesitation, leap from the bath and fling myself into the arms of the first person I found. A table holding the inevitable tin water jug, basin and soap dish stood by one wall, while across from it, in its entire stately splendor, sat a massive commode called a "thunder box." It was freshly painted in white enamel—too freshly painted, I discovered, as I tried to get unstuck the first time I used it. After some panic and a lot of painful struggling, I freed myself, only to have Mike inform me that I was following in the seat of greatness, as it were. Years ago, a member of European royalty found herself in the same horrible situation, only she was glued to a bathtub. The tub, with the royal imprint, was later auctioned for a large sum of money! The lack of plumbing, once my thunder box was dry, didn't worry me in the least, except that I developed a nervous cough, for when Suleiman, our sweeper, appeared outside my bathroom door, he always coughed before he tried it. If I coughed back, he went away until later.

Contrary to custom, Mike and I had our large meal at midday, and after our evening bath sat down in dressing gowns to a light supper of cheese, toast, chips or an omelet. Ghulam, the cook, took a long time to become used to this informal way of living. For many years, his Sahibs and Memsahibs, arrayed in full evening dress, had ploughed through four- and five-course dinners. But he, along with the other servants, learned to like it, as it meant they said their goodnight salaams early and left for home, where they sat outside their mud houses. Surrounded by their families and neighbours, they talked of the strange goings on in the big bungalow by Bisundapur village.

During the monsoon, the insects came by the millions. Attracted by the lights, they poured in to fall in our drinks and down our necks and to buzz in our hair. Looking like a wide black moving staircase, they crept up the walls in never-ending streams, and Suleiman swept up great heaps of them every morning. On nights when they were at their worst, our bathwater was black with them. I just jumped in, insects and all. Nights like these we spent reading in bed in the shelter of our mosquito nets. Frogs of every shape and size, from tiny ones to large fat ones with wide stripes down their backs, shared our house. I once spent an interesting half hour watching one shed its skin. Frogs attract snakes, so every evening Suleiman crept about the bungalow gathering the frogs up in a butterfly net and taking his squirming, wriggling load out to dump over the riverbank. I had one special friend he wasn't allowed to touch, a dear little green frog who appeared every evening in a certain spot on my dressing table and sat watching me do my hair.

Some days we were visited by huge orange-coloured spiders that raced across the room at an incredible speed, waving long feelers. From my perch high up on a chair, I watched Hamid and Mike chase them with sticks. After they were killed, I found, on closer inspection, that legs as thick as matchsticks supported their fat, loathsome bodies.

Let the insects come by the millions, let even centipedes, spiders and scorpions invade our home, which they often did, but Heaven protect me from snakes, little ones, big ones, harmless or poisonous. Until I was safely tucked beneath our net at night, I was forever on the alert, expecting to find a krait in my bathroom or a cobra doing a dance in the living room. The roof of the veranda didn't extend to the very end of the bungalow, and here, at the end, our beds were placed. Each night we slept out under the stars. I learned to ignore the eerie howling and wailing of the jackals, the incessant barking of the pariah dogs and the drums from the Brahmin village over the wall. It took time, though, to fall asleep accompanied by all these strange new sounds, and one night, as I lay listening to the drums and weird chanting, I grew more uneasy and sleep refused to come. As the drums grew louder and faster and the chanting bordered on a hysterical note, I woke Mike up and, in the best offhand manner I could muster, asked, "They wouldn't do anything silly, would they? You know, come over the wall or something like that?"

Mike raised himself up on one elbow and looked at me sleepily. "Who wouldn't do what?"

"That noise," I answered, "those people in the Brahmin village, they sound like they're on the warpath."

Mike sat up in bed, listened, and looking suddenly serious and concerned, sang in a loud voice, "Fee fi fo fum, I smell the blood of an Englishman," then turned over and went to sleep.

Each morning I wakened early, with the delicious feeling of having a whole unhurried day stretching before me, my very own day free of household and cooking responsibilities, a day to do with as I pleased. My only chores were to check the boiling of the drinking water and milk and tell Ghulam what we wanted for our meals. I wrote letters, browsed through the hundreds of books in the den or climbed up broad steps to the roof of the veranda and watched the people who lived in the Brahmin village over the wall.

Waiting by the gate at the end of the driveway for Mike to come home from the office, I watched the people returning from the city with their baskets and bundles balanced upon their heads. Men strode by carrying long lathis or canes. Some had just come back from bathing in the river, and their wet dhotis hung over the lathis and dried in the sun as they walked along. Women, who always walked a few paces behind, followed some. The women, except on festive occasions, wore drab saris, but many of them were beautiful and all had a walk a Power's model would envy. They gave me shy salaams. Overladen ekkas carts rattled by, the poor ponies' bodies covered with sores and their bent legs stumbling over the rough road. Their owners loved nothing better than a race with another ekha filled with too many passengers. The men beat the horses unmercifully, laughing and shouting with glee as they tore up the road. After lunch and a rest, I bathed, dressed and lay flat on the carpet in the drawing room listening to records. The Strauss waltzes always brought the swallows. They swooped gracefully in and out of the veranda and finally right into the room. As the beautiful music poured forth, they flew in rhythm until the record ended and they darted out and away.

As I lay gazing idly at the turning fans, I wondered what time it was at home and what people were doing. Were they just rushing to work or away from it? As much as I longed to see everyone again, I knew also that I wouldn't change this life for anything. I was never bored, never rushed or lonely, and I never wanted to leave.

It was some time before I got wise to the fact that Hamid retired to a string bed behind a mango tree each morning after breakfast, and there he slept until lunchtime, while the others did his work. Hamid had been a bachelor's servant for too long, and he never did forgive me for marrying Mike and disturbing his own lazy life. I spied his large horny feet sticking out from behind the tree by the well and, prodding him awake, I led him back to the bungalow. Pointing to the silver said my newly learned words "Saf karo"—clean. It was a long time before I became used to being waited on. It somehow didn't seem quite right for me to order around men old enough to be my father, and I often had to stop myself from telling them that they may as well go home, as there didn't seem to be anything more to do at the moment.

The cookhouse, thirty-odd feet from the bungalow, was Ghulam's domain. Here he prepared beautifully cooked meals on a primitive stove of brick and mortar in which he burned charcoal and coke. Clad in a string vest, an old pair of pyjama-like trousers and a fur hat, he made burning hot curries each Sunday, starting to prepare them the day before and grinding each spice by hand. These Sunday curries were a ritual and always consumed with ice-cold beer. While Ghulam watched from behind the curtains for our reaction, we ate plates heaped high with mutton curry, rice palao, dahl and large crisp popadums. The hot chapattis—great flat pancake shaped discs of unleavened bread, we tore off in pieces and used in place of forks and spoons. Dishes of spicy mango chutney, hot pickled onions and fresh radishes and green onions from the garden completed the meal. Stuffed with food and beer, we fell onto our beds and slept it off until teatime, an English tea of sandwiches and cakes, dull and uninteresting, I always found, after our Indian lunch.

The shopper who called at our bungalow each morning for our orders before cycling to the bazaar was a short, sturdy Hindu named Dukharan. The company had employed him for many years, starting as cat boy when he was but a child, in charge of Yeld Sahib's Siamese cats. Whenever the bungalow stood empty, Dukharan looked after it, keeping the white ants down and the carpets from rotting during the rains. I liked him on the spot for his sense of humour and twinkling brown eyes, and although he spoke only Hindustani, he and I carried on long conversations and shared many jokes. Dukharan took it upon himself to teach me the language. I learned more from him than I ever did from Mike or my teacher, who came to the bungalow each morning. I nagged at Mike until he agreed to add Dukharan to the bungalow as a bearer.

"You'll never make a decent servant out of him," Mike warned. "He's never waited on a table or served drinks, and he's too old to train now."

But I was determined, and it wasn't long before Dukharan was learning from Ghulam and Hamid. As well-trained servants go, he never did quite make it, but he made up for it in so many other ways. Whenever I fell prey to the tummy upsets one always gets in India, it was Dukharan who fussed over me like a mother hen. The servants blamed any illness on the direction of the wind. "Howa se, Memsahib," they would say. I couldn't see what difference the way the wind blew made to my stomach, but they firmly believed it. I would take some vile medicine and go to bed and lie shivering and feeling very sorry for myself. Dukharan's worried face would appear around my door.

"Taklief, Memsahib?"

"Yes, Dukharan, it's my stomach." Two words I quickly learned were "Trouble" and "Stomach." If a servant wanted leave, it was usually because he had trouble in his stomach or, as he put it, his wife had a baby in hers.

"Howa se," Dukharan would promptly say and disappear. Returning a short while later with a hot water bottle, he would place it at my feet, fluff up the pillows and tuck me in before going out to squat by my door.

"Bless you, Dukharan," I often thought. "You may serve soup with your thumb in it, but I wouldn't change you for all the best-trained servants in India."

The man who filled our baths and drew all the water for the cookhouse and bungalow was a thin, grumpy-looking Hindu named Gajada. The others always teased poor Gajada. I felt sorry for him, especially when I watched him hauling up great goat skins brimming with water from the well or staggering along with weighty kerosene tins full, but long after Mike had laid on running cold water in the bungalow and around the compound, Gajada ignored the taps and continued to pull by hand. It was plain to see that very little kindness had ever been shown this ugly old man. Mike teased me by saying that Gajada deliberately cut himself while chopping wood, just so I could bandage him up. Hardly a week went by when Dukharan didn't come to me and say, "Gajada hai," with a look that said, "The old fool has done it again." I would go to my first aid cupboard and gather up Dettol, cotton wool and bandages before going out to find Gajada squatting by the veranda gazing mournfully down at his foot. Taking it in my hand, I would find amongst the blood and filth a stone tied on top of the wound with a dirty piece of cloth. After I'd cleansed and bandaged things up, he would for a second reward me with one of his rare smiles, then limp off, only to return in a few days with another injury covered by another stone.

Aziz and Sagir, our two Muslim drivers, had assistants to help wash the car. Aziz was tall, fat and lazy, and he always stood by, hands behind his back, stomach well out, directing operations. Sagir was a hard worker but had the unfortunate habit of always doing the wrong thing. He was forever being fired by Mike, only to be forgiven and rehired in the morning. In fact, he became so used to it that I'm sure each time he was sacked, he went home and caught up on a lot of chores or went to a movie, before appearing early the next day to be reinstated!

Mahadeo, the head mali or gardener, was a small Hindu with an immense turban. He always appeared to me as just a turban with a pair of thin brown legs running along beneath it. He bossed four regular gardeners and a bird-scaring woman. One of the malis resembled a rat, and all his children looked like rats, too.

"He eats rats, Memsahib," Dukharan told me with a chuckle. "You can tell by looking at him."

Mahadeo tended over 130 fruit trees, grapefruit, lemon, lime and guava, tangelo, papaya, banana, leechee and mango. Five hundred strawberry plants were nursed along but, strawberries being difficult to grow in India, the most fruit we got was about sixty berries. We served them to guests one day with homemade ice cream, pretending this was our daily taking. In the kitchen garden by the cookhouse, Mahadeo grew every kind of Indian and European vegetable, and it was because of him that we enjoyed nearly the whole year round a lush green lawn.

Besides the odd dishwasher, one who was the image of a camel ("He was once bitten by a camel, Memsahib," Dukharan said), two night watchmen and a shopper, these people kept our bungalow and garden running smoothly. As my Hindustani improved, so I learned of the way they lived, their joys and fears, and, came to recognize and sort out their numerous children and relatives.

7

Carpets

"How would you like a job in one of the hottest parts of India, away from so-called civilization but full of interest and taking you amongst the real people of India,—the village folk?" This was the gist of a letter Mike received just after his 17th birthday from the father of a school friend, offering him a position with an English firm of carpet manufacturers.

Until 1912 the secret of carpet weaving in the Mirzapur district was solely in the hands of the descendants of weavers who began their craft during the reign of Akbar the Great in the 16th century. They tacked, "Kalin Bap" after their name, which literally means, "Father of Carpets." These families were all Mohammedan but with the increased demand for these beautiful rugs, it was essential that the business expand. So it became necessary for all members of the community to learn the craft. Today there is not a single caste or class, which is not represented in the Mirzapur weaving community. Indigo was the main industry of Mirzapur until a stable, cheap blue dye was developed in the late 19th century and the Indigo business was ruined. Around this time, Harry Brandford, then a boy of sixteen, negotiated to supply a British company with an order of hand made carpets. From this trial order developed one of the largest cottage industries in the world. The orders came into the main mail office of the E. Hill and Company office at Mirzapur. The factory lay on the north side of the Ganges at Khamariah, isolated except by boat for six months of the year. At the beginning of the cold weather, a pontoon bridge was laid across the river and then dismantled with the advent of the monsoon.

The Khamariah factory contained the dye houses, a yarn storage warehouse and design rooms. Clipping, carving and carpet finishing was done at the factory. Then, each rug was inspected by one of the European managers before being baled and shipped. The carpets themselves were woven in the weavers' houses in the surrounding villages. Loom inspectors made weekly tours of the villages to see that all was going according to plan. The Managing Director's bungalow, occupied by Bill Wallis and his family, sat in the same compound.

Mike promised to take me on a tour of the carpet world, and early one morning we set off for the village of Hussenipur. The houses belonging to the weavers were made of brick and were sturdier than the mud and wattle huts of other villagers. Stopping the car, Mike and I got out beside a long low-whitewashed house. A man came running up to us and made us welcome with a deep salaam.

"Salaam, Udai," Mike said and turning to me, he went on, "Mary, I'd like you to meet the loom owner of the largest carpet hand loom in the world. And he's a thief into the bargain!" Udai and I salaamed one another and as we walked towards his house, I asked Mike for an explanation. "It's a fact," Mike replied, "Udai is a Hindu pasi by caste. They're normally swineherds and thieves by profession and usually considered pretty low on the Hindu social register. Udai and I are old friends, however. I trust him implicitly and look upon him as a brother. A number of years ago," Mike went on, "we received so many requests from the ruling Princes of India to weave them outlandish and seamless carpets for their palaces, that we decided to erect a loom capable of fulfilling all orders. Udai's two loom beams are made of steel cylinders and can weave a seamless carpet up to fifty feet in width and one hundred and fifty feet long."

As we entered the house, the sound of dull hammering met our ears. Mike explained that weavers were hammering down the weft strands on the carpet fabric. There were three huge fifteen-foot rolls being woven on this steel monster. These were destined, Mike told me, for the New York market. Thirty men and boys sat on a long seat on one side of the rugs, weaving away. Some were tying the knots forming the pile tufts, some were drawing the weft threads and others sheared the pile. Still others were hammering with heavy metal combs. Hundreds of balls of yarn in every imaginable colour hung above their heads. I sat down beside one of the weavers and was amazed at the speed of his flying fingers as he tied the knots and cut the yarn with a heavy curved knife. Occasionally, he referred to a working design that hung behind him. More often, he appeared to be weaving from a sixth sense.

Stooping low, we entered other huts that held smaller wooden looms. "This is an old Persian design." Mike pointed to a half finished carpet of Royal blue, reds and wine. "It will have over one million hand tied knots in it before it is completed."

We looked at designs in Chinese, Swedish Modern and North African. French Aubusson rugs in soft pastel shades glowed upon the looms in many houses and they let me clumsily tie a few knots in a rug Mike was having made for my dad. The people all gathered to see us leave. Standing on one leg, and leaning forward as they salaamed, they looked like they were doing the sailor's hornpipe. They watched us until we were out of sight.

Gradually the rains ended, and the few Europeans who lived close-by returned from their hill and home leaves. Just past Bisundapur village, Sylvia and Henri Cros lived in the office compound with their small son Alain. The Croses' bungalow, larger than ours, also looked out over the river. But the high bank had been slowly eaten away over the years, until the edge of the veranda was only a few feet from where the bank fell steeply away to the water. Sylvia was younger than I, a pretty English girl with dark curly hair. Henri was French and Russian, slim, and with a sallow complexioned. His moods varied from high spirits to low depression. "These people," was a favourite expression of Henri's. "These people," annoyed and irritated him. "These people," were lazy, incompetent and useless. Actually, he was very fond of them, but when he was sunk low in one of his moods, he would hunch his shoulders, stick out his lower lip and spread his hands in typical French fashion, and blame it all on "These people."

In a wisteria-covered bungalow across the road from ours lived Wilfred and Elaine Oakley. Tall, red faced with sandy hair and a mustache, Wilfred belonged to a competing carpet firm. Elaine, almost as tall as Wilfred, reminded me strongly of Victoria, one of my friends from

Vancouver. She had with a similar sense of humour. Dukharan adored Elaine, and would go running up the drive to meet her as she came sailing down for morning coffee.

A mile down the road toward Mirzapur city, and just past the village of Fatahar, Wilfred's two assistants lived in a stone bungalow in a huge riverside compound. Alan Randall from Yorkshire was an immense young man with dark curly hair. David Logan, also tall and dark, was Scottish. We all excitedly awaited his fiancée Natalie, who was flying out from Edinburgh in November to marry him. Even before I met Natalie, I had a strong feeling that in her, I would find the friendship of Lee, Victoria and Ethel, friendships I greatly missed. Soon after she arrived, David brought Natalie to our house for dinner. Blonde, attractive and my own age, Natalie and I formed a lasting friendship on the spot.

8

pregnant

WHEN I FIRST ARRIVED, Suleiman gave me a gift of luridly painted clay dolls for fertility. These must have been effective. One afternoon, Aziz drove me down to the Mission to see Evelyn Neech, our doctor. Evelyn was an American and married to Alan, our tall handsome Padre. "It will be around July 10th, Mary," Evelyn said.

"July? Then she will be born in the hills, we'd both like a girl," I said. "I'm going to Mussoorie, do you know it, Evelyn?" I asked.

"Yes, well, Alan and I met there at Language School. Landour Community Hospital is very well run and you'll have the best of care."

"Would you like to look around our hospital before you leave?" I wanted to very much as I had often wondered what went on behind the walls of the long brick building by the Mission gates. At the hospital, people looked up at Evelyn with adoring eyes as she adjusted their bandages and checked their charts, all the time re-assuring them quietly in her excellent Hindustani.

"Here's an interesting case, Mary," said Evelyn.

She led me into a small room where a woman lay alone. I tried not to show the shock I felt at her appearance. She was painfully thin with huge staring eyes.

"Her sister brought her in," Evelyn explained, "she was deserted by her husband and lay starving and ill for weeks."

Evelyn took her hand and we stood looking down at this pitiful, barely living skeleton.

"When she was first admitted," Evelyn went on, "she could only open her mouth a quarter of an inch and the stench from her was overpowering. Indians are accustomed to the worst odours, but this was too much and the other patients asked me to move her."

"Whatever did you do to help her?" I asked.

"I irrigated," Evelyn replied, "and found she was full of maggots, the result of lying in her own filth for so long. She'll be alright now!"

We visited the maternity ward where unbelievably young mothers proudly displayed their tiny babies with heads no larger than oranges.

"Are these people patients?" I asked, pointing to the dozen-odd women who sat on top or beside the beds, some lying fast asleep beneath.

"No," Evelyn grinned, "They are the patients' relations. Only the Christians will eat the food prepared in the hospital cookhouse, the others bring their relations to cook for them. Come out onto the veranda, they are preparing meals now."

Squatting by charcoal fires, people were busily cooking food and gossiping with loud voices. As the noise of their chatter, and the strong aroma of a dozen different curries drifted through the open windows, I wondered how on earth the ill ever managed to recover at all. Thanking Evelyn, I waved goodbye. Aziz drove me home where I found Mike pacing anxiously up and down the veranda.

Mike went about in a daze and Sylvia began teaching me to knit. I spent hours labouring over a grimy piece of knitting, unraveling and starting over again until Mike complained that every time he looked at me, I was ripping it out. Wasn't I ever going to master it? I did, and knitted him a yellow cable-knit pullover. Dukharan, proud of my accomplishment, refused to trust the dhobi and washed it himself. It was hanging four feet long, and dripping wet over a towel rack when Mike discovered it!

Like most husbands when their first baby is on its way, Mike had to get used to my odd cravings and changing moods. First it was peanuts and from them the baby's nickname originated. Then it was boiled sweets. All I could think of was boiled sweets, like the lovely acidy pear drops you buy in England. I wanted them badly. When the shopper came for our list of supplies from Allahabad, I added two pounds of boiled sweets to it. Allahabad is sixty miles away from Mirzapur. As the man always went by train, he didn't appear with his purchases until early the following morning. Boiled sweets! I yearned for them. Mentally I ate the whole two pounds before dinner. I went to bed to dream of them. I was on the veranda early the next morning, and while the shopper opened the boxes and Mike checked off the list, I delved through the packages. "Where are my boiled sweets?" I demanded. "Here, Memsahib," and he handed me a grimy bag. I opened it to find a sticky mass of unwrapped sweets.

"You can't eat those," Mike said. "They're not safe, been crawling with flies by the look of them," and he went on checking off the list. I sat down on the edge of the veranda and began to cry.

"My lovely boiled sweets. How could he?"

"Whatever is wrong?" I looked up to find them all staring down in astonishment.

"My boiled sweets, that's what's wrong, I've been waiting and longing for them since yesterday morning."

"But he'll get them on his next trip," Mike explained.

"I can't wait two weeks. I want them now," I wailed and sniffed loudly in my hanky, while Dukharan gave the shopper dirty looks.

So, the man went back to Allahabad. He traveled one hundred and twenty miles to satisfy my craving. I hated myself, but after making such a fuss, I couldn't very well back down. When the shopper returned, I rewarded him handsomely, grabbed the bag. Unable to restrain myself, I ate a whole pound in one afternoon.

During our short stay in Bombay when we were married, we had been offered a Doberman pinscher puppy. While out visiting one evening, our hostess opened the door of a small room to disclose a tiny shivering black and tan pup. I knelt beside her, she jumped up, and snuggled in my neck, making small contented sniffling noises. Mrs. Sadler beamed down at us. "She likes you. I can tell as she usually shies away from strangers. Her previous owner had neglected her, and if you would really like to have her, I'll wire you when I feel she's ready to travel." I wanted to take her away immediately. But we left, after promising to send for her when we received Mrs. Sadler's wire. A month later, we heard that Chipso, as we named her, was ready. Suleiman left to pick her up on his first long journey and his first glimpse of the sea.

We were impatiently waiting on the station platform when the train pulled in and we saw Suleiman leading her from the carriage. Chipso stood looking about her and sniffing. Then like a bolt of lightning, she threw herself at me and up into my arms. The change in her was unbelievable. Her coat shone like satin. Her intelligent soft brown eyes were clear and bright. And she had grown enormously. Rushing back and forth between Mike, Suleiman and me, we finally managed to calm her down enough to get her into the car. Throughout the difficult journey through the bazaar, it was almost impossible to restrain her from leaping over the seat and settling herself in Mike's lap. When we arrived home, she made a quick inspection of the garden and then the drawing room. She parked her bottom on the low settee and stretched her long legs out, looking for all the world as if she had come for tea. She looked at Mike and me in turn, sighed a deep sigh of contentment and fell asleep. She was home.

It was fun having Chipso to fuss over. We took her for long walks, and she formed a fleeting friendship with a little fox that teased her by popping up amongst the crops, playing a form of hide and seek. She walked at our heels through the village with her nose in the air, ignoring the snapping and snarling of the village pi dogs. She seemed to have a well-bred animal's snobbishness. Poor creatures, although they outnumbered her and sounded ferocious and terrifying, she need only bare her teeth and they were off, tumbling over each other to get out of her way, yelping with fright.

Angela and Charles Grubb came to live in the station with their two small children. Everyone made them welcome, too welcome in fact. They possessed the mistaken idea that they could call any time, day or night and stay for hours, disturbing our well loved solitude. Never waiting for the bearer to announce them, they thought it a great joke to creep silently through the dining room and hall, and pop joyously out from behind the curtains upon Mike and me. The popular saying round about was, "We're going to do so and so this evening, come hell, high water, or the Grubbs!" We were all in despair. Even when they didn't turn up, each carrying a sad pale looking child, we never the less expected them to. Our evenings were spoiled anyway.

"What are we going to do, Sylvia? Angela came for coffee yesterday morning, and then again in the evening," I said.

"She was at our place for tea," Sylvia complained. "Henri and I are completely fed up."

Soon, however, we found a solution to the Grubb problem, in our bungalow anyway. I was sitting in the drawing room reading one evening before our baths, when Mike slithered in. Stark naked except for a huge green turban upon his head, he leapt onto the chesterfield and bounded across the floor while the ends of the turban sailed out behind. He was just making a great pirouette into the air, when the curtains parted, and there stood Angela Grubb!

9

Chowkidars & Celebrations

To guard the compound and house, we employed two night watchmen called, "Chowkidars", Mayhi Lal and old Husani. When it became dark, they circled the house with lanterns and carrying long spears, uttering loud shouts and coughs, presumably to keep prowlers away. Mike pointed out to them that the bungalow could easily be robbed on one side, while they were busily coughing and shouting on the other, but it took some time to break them of the habit. Old Husani had been coughing and yelling on the job for years. They were known as the "Bloody Chowkidars," mainly because Mike usually caught them napping or playing cards.

Our chowkidars found themselves in trouble one evening. They neglected to come and investigate when Chipso began barking furiously. Mike rushed out on the veranda yelling, "Where are those bloody chowkidars?" Husani and Mayhi Lal came running up to receive a long lecture on the many reasons Chipso could be barking: mad dogs, snakes, prowlers or any manner of things.

"Han Sahib, we understand." Salaaming deeply, they returned to work. The next night, we were asleep on the veranda with Chipso on her bed beside us. She suddenly leapt up and began barking frantically once more. Around came the chowkidars, and so it went on until Mike suddenly shot up in bed and hollered "Hut jao, you bloody chowkidars!" And they went scurrying away across the lawn.

"What did you do that for?" I asked, "Last night you insisted they come every time Chipso barked, and now you tell them to go away."

"Well, I'm fed up," he shouted. "Every time I open my eyes, what do I see? A pair of skinny legs and a lantern going by."

He dove under the net, lit a cigarette, and lay back puffing furiously. Again, we settled off to sleep, with Chipso wrapped up in a blanket, when a pi dog crept up and attacked her. As she tried to free herself and fight back, the pi dog disappeared into the bungalow. I was screaming, Mike was tangled up in the mosquito net, shouting and swearing while Chipso went wild with rage—no chowkidars! Ripping the net in shreds, Mike rushed off to the front of the bungalow, and found Husani and Mayhi Lal on the veranda, each pushing one the other: "You go," "No, you go."

I was sitting up in bed holding Chipso, when the three of them came around the corner. Mike, white with anger, grabbed a long curtain pole and ordered, "Follow me, men." He marched into the house. Old Husani followed him with his spear ready, while Mayhi Lal, having lost his weapon in the confusion, carefully closed the door and stood holding it. Meanwhile twenty-odd other doors and windows about the house remained wide open. I listened to them poking about inside, under beds, behind doors and in closets. Then I heard a noise by my bed and a low warning growl from Chipso. I saw the pi dog slink out and disappear into the darkness.

"It's alright, Mike," I called. "He's gone."

Releasing Chipso, I entered Mike's dressing room to find him, hands behind his back, striding up and down before the two men and pouring forth a torrent of Hindustani. Stopping before the men, Mike shouted, "What are you anyway?"

In small voices, they replied, "We're chowkidars."

"Then you're sacked," Mike roared, and returned to bed. I waited for his anger to abate and then ventured,

"Poor men, I wonder how many children Mayhi Lal has, Mike?"

Silence.

"Husani is so old and I heard yesterday that his wife is ill."

Silence. As a pair of skinny legs and a lantern drifted by, I sighed deeply and said, "I wonder if they have any money put by?"

Mike fidgeted a bit, and then finally said, "All right, I'll keep them, but I'm not telling them now. I want some sleep."

I should have known that parting with his servants didn't come easily to Mike. The only one we ever did get rid of was Hamid, and he really sacked himself.

For a long time we had been trying to let him go, but put it off, despite his lazy ways and his gloominess. One morning while in a temper, he informed us he was quitting. Packing his tin trunk, he left our service. We were pleased and promptly took on Ghulam's brother Pir Mohammed, a kindly looking man with a deep comforting voice. He, too, was a cook and took over Ghulam's duties whenever Ghulam was away. Our house was happier for Hamid's absence. Two weeks later, we received a letter from Hamid, written by the village scribe:

Honoured Sir,
It is with due respect and humble submission that I beg to lay these few miserable lines before your good self. I pray and beseech that you will once again take my worthless self back into your honour's service. The reason for my rash action is that for the last three weeks I have been suffering from insanity. Praying that your honour will grant me this boon and blessing.

I am,
Your humble servant,
Hamid bearer.

We didn't.

November brought my birthday, and a lovely old emerald and diamond ring from Mike. For many weeks, I had noticed a general cleaning up going on. Not only was our bungalow freshly colour-washed, and the shutters re-done in green, but every mud hut in the village was white-washed. All the shrines were painted and the grounds tidied up. Mike told me that Diwali, the most beautiful of all Hindu festivals, was approaching. I looked forward to it, secretly wondering why I wasn't told more about it. On the day of Diwali, the servants crept about furtively, and I received a polite brush off whenever I tried to find out what they did to celebrate.

"Just what do they do?" I asked.

"Oh, nothing much," Mike replied, "They just tidy up their houses in preparation for the cold weather and have a sort of festival."

But something was going on, and no one was telling me. During breakfast, down the drive came a man Mike called "the man of God." He was an Indian Christian, and caretaker of our little church. Whenever Alan, our Padre, could manage a service, the caretaker took around the notice to various bungalows for the church members to sign. He spoke no English, and carried out his duties with great dignity. Standing stiffly to attention while I read and signed the notice, he carefully took it from me, salaamed and stalked off up the drive. But I knew his dreadful secret, I knew, that sometimes, when Alan was away, the man of God kept his goats in the vestry!

It was still light when we drove to church that evening. I had the peculiar feeling that the servants couldn't wait for us to leave. Around trees or behind bushes, I caught glimpses of the malis watching us go. The church stood at the beginning of Fatahar village, and after Mike parked the car, we got out to wait for Alan and the Missahibs to arrive from the mission. The jeep came bouncing through the village, arrived in a cloud of dust, jerked to a stop. The Missahibs piled out. Then Alan, stretching out a bare leg and a bare foot encased in a sandal, unfolded himself and squeezed out, disclosing that under his sombre black robe, he wore shorts. We chatted awhile, and then crept inside. In the hot weather, the fans that hung from the ceiling did little to relieve the heat. In the winter, it was cold and draughty, but we loved St. John's and looked forward to the services. We sat in the quiet church, the Missahibs on one side, and Mike and I on the other.

"Who plays the organ, Mike?" I asked.

"No one, it hasn't been played for years. The organist had a nervous breakdown and had to leave the country."

I looked at the little organ.

"No wonder," I said, out of the corner of my mouth.

"What do you mean?" Mike asked, softly.

"Well, look at the seat, it tips forward about 45 degrees!"

I visualized a little Missahib playing the harmonium, furiously pumping like mad with her feet while her bottom slipped farther and farther down the seat. I could see her in my mind's eye, neck getting red, giving a great heave against the pedals, settling herself back up on her precarious perch, pumping and playing away, only to begin slowly slipping forward again. It was enough to give anyone nerves, I decided, and got an uncontrollable fit of giggles just as Alan strode up the aisle to begin the service for his congregation of five.

We started off on an unfamiliar hymn. Mike, as usual, sang loud and lustily while I followed meekly a few beats behind. Among a large congregation, you may work your lips pretending to sing while not making a sound. In a company of five, you either start and carry on, or not begin at all. Alan, whenever felt he was getting out of his depth, broke off, and did the usual things a minister does, while we struggled on. Our voices poured out through the easy parts, weakened, stumbled and grew strong again. All of a sudden, Mike bellowed forth some very sour notes and I followed suit. Succumbing to a fit of giggles, we silently stood throughout that long, long hymn: faces red, stomachs aching from suppressed laughter while the Missahibs in thin quavering voices sang bravely on.

The service in Alan's quiet voice was held against a background of weird noises from Fatahar village. Drums clanked, dogs yelped, and villagers gossiped in loud voices near the village well. I glanced across at the Missahibs, erect in cotton dresses and felt hats. As I watched them I thought, what great courage they possessed in leaving their homes and families to travel thousands of miles to devote their lives in teaching and nursing these people. They did not live an easy life. They worked long hours at thankless tasks, and were criticized by the people, even those of their own country and faith. They were even begrudged a few weeks rest in the cool of the hills.

After service, Mike turned the car away from home.

"Where are we going?" I asked.

I wanted to get back and watch the festival, but we drove through the jungle for miles until it began to grow dark and we headed for home. Driving up strange streets, past the sweepers' hovels, past the Mohammedan cemetery, we made our way back to the bungalow where, just before we reached the drive-way I was told to close my eyes. The car stopped.

"Now." Mike said.

I opened my eyes to behold a fairyland! Against a velvet sky, the entire bungalow was outlined in soft flickering lights. They lined the drive. Over the gateway, boughs were bent to form an arch where hundreds of lights glowed.

"Oh, it's beautiful," I breathed, scarcely daring to talk, lest it should all disappear. Never before had I realized the harshness of an electric light, not until I saw the effect of thousands of lighted wicks as they floated in little clay saucers of oil. I got out of the car and wandered down the drive. The servants, malis, men from the office and village stood about in groups quietly chatting. Their white teeth flashed as they salaamed me and each dark eye watched my reaction to my first Diwali.

"Oh, it's beautiful!" I said again as we stood on the riverside and watched the lights floating down the river. A huge orange moon laid a silvery path on Mother Ganges' quiet waters.

"So this is Diwali." I said to Mike.

"Yes, darling, this is Diwali, and no matter how many Diwalis you see, the thrill will always be the same, for you can never quite get enough of it and you can never fully describe it no matter how you try," he said.

As Christmas drew near, Sylvia, Natalie and I met in Elaine's bungalow to begin planning for the children's party at the Mirzapur Club. Elaine and Sylvia, complete with list, drove to Allahabad to shop for toys and sweets while Natalie and I decorated the club. The dhobis, or launderers, scrubbed their donkeys until they shone. They strapped clean blankets on their backs and brought them to the club on the day of the party for the children to ride upon. The party, held two days before Christmas, was a great success. After games, races and rides, we all trooped across to Elaine's bungalow for movies and tea. Elaine's house stood in a huge compound and she is the only person I have ever met who had an elephant in her garden and couldn't find it!

"Where's the elephant?" we all asked.

"Around somewhere," Elaine replied, "it was over by the well this morning, but I can't seem to see it now."

Tea was over. The elephant was found and ridden upon by excited children, watched by nervous mothers. We all gathered in the hall to wait for Santa Claus. Far away, we heard the jingling of bells and Mike, dressed as Santa Claus, drove up in an ekka and jumped out with a bulging pillowcase of toys over his shoulder.

Christmas Eve we held a dinner party in our bungalow. A snowy white cloth covered the table, and each goblet held expertly folded napkins in the shape of animals and flowers. We dined by candlelight while a fire burned cozily in the grate. A small gift for each guest lay by each plate. The turkeys, roasted in covered tins above charcoal fires, were perfect and Ghulam made a jelly similar to cranberry from the flower of the Petwa bush. Fresh vegetables were plentiful. Green beans, peas, brussels sprouts and everything for a salad. Finishing off with mince pie and ice cream, we all staggered into the drawing room to relax before a roaring fire with our coffee and liqueurs.

Christmas morning, Mike and I opened our presents around the tree while the servants peeked through the curtains. I undid clumsily wrapped gifts from Mike, exquisite gauzy scarves from Benares spilled out, shot with gold and silver. They looked too delicate to wear. "Here, you've forgotten this," and Mike tossed over a small parcel. Inside was a beautiful diamond cluster ring. The servants, unable to restrain their curiosity, were right amongst the tissue paper and ribbons, almost as excited as we were.

Every year the company held a party on our lawn for the weavers and village children. As we drove out the gateway to church, they were already gathering on the road. When we arrived back, great crowds were waiting. Husani and Mayhi Lal tried to keep them back by a rope stretched across the driveway. On the lawn, I watched the office clerks and malis placing sweet-meats on banana leaves in long lines across the grass, while the Conjuror unpacked his box of tricks on the veranda. The signal was given and the rope taken down. With a great roar, over four hundred children burst into the compound. I watched in amazement as they stepped carefully over the flowerbeds and around the rose bushes. They walked in perfect order and sat cross-legged in front of the sweets. Apart from the noise, they behaved well and I wondered what condition our garden would have been in after an invasion of four hundred Canadian children. They watched wide-eyed while the conjuror entertained them. They roared with laughter when he produced annas and rupees from a little boy's bottom.

When the show was over, they carefully wrapped their sweet-meats in the banana leaves, and salaaming wildly, they left, leaving the compound neat and tidy. All the clerks and many of the weavers came to salaam us and to hang heavily scented garlands around our necks. Mike, with garlands up to his ears, sat in the den with stacks of money piled before him, giving out the baksheesh or bonus. In order, the staff waited on the veranda. Ghulam first, Dukharan, Pir Mohammed and so on, down through the malis, drivers, dhobi and barber. Everyone who had had anything to do with us in the past months, turned up with the hope that the good humour Christmas always produced in the Sahib would benefit them in the form of baksheesh. They were all rewarded. Then Mike looked up to find a strange man standing before him.

"Who are you?" Mike asked.

"The grave digger from the local cemetery," the man replied.

"When I die, old man, it is my wish that I be burned and cast into the Mother Ganges," Mike told him, and then gave him a rupee anyway.

Outside there was suddenly the most dreadful row I have ever heard. I jumped and covered my ears while Chipso promptly wet on the carpet and shivering with fright, crawled under the lounge.

"Whatever is that?" I asked.

"Molar's band, isn't it awful?"

We went outside. There, in a group, stood Suleiman's father with his band made up of his four sons. Bagpipes wailed, horns screeched, cymbals crashed and the smallest boy pounded on a drum as they played over and over, the one and only tune they knew.

"For God's sake! Do they have to play so loudly?" Mike demanded and rushed inside for their baksheesh. Raising his hand, he made a short speech saying how much we had enjoyed it, gave out the money and bade them good day. He had just poured his beer and put his feet up, when they started again, even louder, and with more gusto, for hadn't the Sahib said how much he and the Memsahib had enjoyed it? Mike held his head and said,

"You know, they call our Christmas 'Burra Din' which means 'big day.' But when Molar and his outfit turn up, it means just what it says, a big din."

He went outside and, taking Molar to one side, talked to him.

"What did you say?" I asked, as I watched Molar and his band troop up the drive. With a fiendish look on his face, Mike replied, "I told him to go over to the Cros Sahib's bungalow as I felt sure they would enjoy it if they played to them for awhile!"

As I undressed for bed that night, I looked at the garlands lying over the chair, their lovely flowers already bruised and dying. I thought of all the hard-earned annas that had gone into them, and of the way the servants and everyone had worked to make our day a happy one. I realized how very much they had all come to mean to me, and what a lovely Christmas day it had turned out to be. With Molar's tune repeating over and over in my head, I fell asleep.

10

the garden and the hostess

In January, our garden was at its best. Lining the driveway in front, there were Sweet Peas on one side and Hollyhocks on the other. In front of these were Snapdragons, Larkspur, Stocks, Cineraria and African Daisies. Circular beds of Canna Lilies like giant flames of fire in orange and red were planted near the entrance. Huge spreading bushes of Poinsettias grew all over the compound. Our bedroom doors opened out onto a beautiful rose garden that was Mike's joy. On the riverside, surrounding trees and in separate beds, were Violets, Pansies and Asters. Dahlias filled the beds running the entire length of the lawn by the riverbank. Hedges of Bougainvillea ranged from pale pink to deep rose and magenta. There were Magnolia trees and bushes of Gardenia. I looked back to the days my dates had shyly presented me with Gardenia corsages that cost them a good part of their precious wages. Here, Mahadeo filled bowls with them and placed them about the house. Every morning, one end of the veranda was a riot of colour. I spent a good half-hour arranging flowers in a dozen different vases. I especially loved one corner of the garden. The hedge of Bougainvillea met a towering hedge of Petria, that beautiful flower of pale mauve. Behind this grew another hedge whose flowers were similar to a massive Honeysuckle in deep orange and yellow. Two small Palms grew nearby. We often had tea outside and sat watching the peacocks as they came over the roof of the servant's quarters and down to the riverbank. They strutted up and down, spreading their gorgeous tails for us to admire. We ate piping hot scones, home made bread with jelly made from our own guavas. Dukharan quietly arranged the table, setting it with the old silver tea service and the Worcester china tea set from Mike's old home in England. Bees lazily hummed and brightly coloured butterflies of all shapes flitted in and out among the flowers.

"Look! There's a mongoose!" And the small animal would peek out from under a hedge, twitching its pink nose and coming nearer to the table for a tidbit. An iguana lived in our garden as well. This was a large lizard about four feet long with a purple forked tongue that darted in and out with lightning speed. His name was Albert and Chipso loved to chase him across the lawn. Albert was far too fast for her. We had a sneaking suspicion that Chipso purposely kept just behind him. We were sure she wouldn't have known what to do with this miniature dinosaur if she did happen to catch him. The servants warned us against Albert.

"He's bad, Memsahib, we call him 'bees cobra,' which means he's worse than twenty cobras put together, a look from him will kill!"

We liked old Albert, for all that, and between him and the mongoose, our compound was kept free of snakes.

Under the jackfruit tree stood an old birdbath and the garden was teeming with a tremendous variety of birds, of which the Seven Sisters were the least attractive. Their grey feathers were ruffled and untidy looking, and they were forever arguing. There were orange and black striped Hoopoo Birds, with their long beaks and high crests, Blue Jays, Golden Orioles, bright green Parakeets and Mynahs. The most entertaining, we found, were the large, cheeky, black Crows. They loved to "swear" and talk back to us. One day, while Chipso was busy with a bone, a crow flew down and pecked her bottom. When she turned around in indignation, it snitched her bone and flew away with it.

Another day, on hearing a terrible noise, I ran out to find a wild cat the size of Chipso being chased by hundreds of angry screeching birds. They flew at him, pecked him, and finally drove him clear out of the garden and into the club compound.

Dozens of grey squirrels ran about freely. They were actually tree rats and very destructive to a garden. Cages were placed about and I came upon them full of panicky frightened squirrels.

"Poor things, do they destroy them, Mike?"

"Oh, they just take them away," he replied.

But I knew that they surely must kill them. So, when no one was looking, I would stand innocently by, flip up the door with my foot, and let them all out.

"Never, at, anytime, allow a goat to come into our garden," Mike warned me. "They can ruin everything in no time. Call a mali and have it chased out immediately."

I promised to do just that, as I had seen the state he got into whenever a goat as much as looked at the gate. Goats were caught and locked up in a little walled compound until their weeping owners came to claim them. I let these out too, if I had the chance, and sent them galloping off up the street. One day, while sitting on the veranda writing, I looked up to see a goat appear by the gate and trot down the drive. Jumping up, I waved my arms wildly, and tried to chase it out. It ignored me and proceeded to munch on the snapdragons. I rushed around the bungalow calling for Mahadeo.

"Jaldi, Mahadeo, jaldi!"

Not knowing the word for "goat," I gesticulated like mad and ran on ahead. Hitching up his dhoti, Mahadeo ran after me, and I pointed dramatically up the driveway—it was empty. Mahadeo looked up the drive, back at me, and up the drive again. Oh, how frustrating, not being able to speak the language! Shaking his head, Mahadeo turned away and left me standing with a weak grin on my face. I went back to the veranda and sat down, I must ask Mike the word for goat, I thought, and then I looked up and it was there again. Jumping off the veranda, I flew around to call Mahadeo again, "Mahadeo, Mahadeo, Jaldi!" and rushed off at top speed with him close behind. The driveway was empty! Mahadeo looked at me, his eyes full of sympathy and went back to weeding the strawberries.

The cold weather passed pleasantly and gradually the days became warmer. We planned to have a large party before I left for the hills and preparations similar to those preceding Christmas began, especially in the cookhouse. Ghulam was in his element, and assured us that he would take care of everything. So, apart from a few special orders, he was given a free hand. He disappeared into the cookhouse and Pir Mohammed took over his duties. Suleiman cleaned the bungalow thoroughly and

Dukharan sent the uniforms to the dhobi, cleaned the silver, polished the glasses, and did a million and one jobs. Tables were placed upon carpets on the lawn with an individual light on each. The carpets in the living room were rolled up, and the floor and veranda were prepared for dancing.

The night of the party, I stood in front of the glass in my dressing room, struggling to dress. All my clothes were two and three inches too small around the waist and impossible to get into, so I was going to wear a sari. In vain, I tried to remember Sylvia's instructions. It had looked so easy. But I was learning that it was not, as I became entangled in yards and yards of silk. How did these women do it? I had often watched them from the riverbank as they waded into the water to bathe. Submerging themselves a few times, they would throw a dry sari around themselves and manage to remove the wet one and don the dry one in a few deft movements. Here I was wrapped up like an Egyptian mummy. When I took a step, I very nearly fell flat on my face. I called Mike for help and he unwound me and started all over again.

"Now begins here. It's most important you begin from the correct side," he said, "You bring it around here, gather it up, tuck it in."

Running around, he gathered, tucked and draped. I was about to ask him how he knew so much about the workings of a sari, when the whole thing fell off and lay in mounds at my feet! Finally, I gave up and sent an SOS to Sylvia who hurried over and dressed me. I went out to greet our guests with my sari fastened together with four great safety pins, and, as I was taller than the average Indian woman, it hung well above my ankles.

Bearers stood by the front, directing the ladies to my dressing room and the men to the guest room by the den. Strange bearers flitted about acting as if they had worked in our bungalow all their lives. There were friends and relations of Ghulam, come to help and get in on the fun. One kept the records going, while others served the drinks. Suleiman and Molar were both on duty, Mahadeo, and his malis stayed behind to watch.

A light stood at one end of the lawn to attract the flying insects away from the table. At the other end, I saw hidden in the shadows, Ghulam and Pir Mohammed busily laying the cloth for dinner.

The women wore some of the most beautiful saris I had ever seen, saris woven in Benares in exquisite shades with wide gold or silver brocade borders. Confined in my rather ordinary sari, I felt as if I were tied up in a sheet and went to meet each guest by crossing the lawn in short jerky steps. I envied these women their graceful way of walking, and thought, once again, how clumsy we Europeans looked in our Western dress. My duties as a hostess over for a moment, I sat and watched them all as they chatted at the various tables, or danced on the veranda. Mike, with a big fat cigar stuck in his teeth, was busy at the bar under the mango tree. He and the other Europeans wore white dinner jackets and black trousers while the Indian men wore formal suits of black.

In a moment, Ghulam appeared by my side, and announced that the food was ready. At his signal, the Burmese gong was rung and the table lighted. Trying to appear as casual as if I served food like this at all my parties, I found it difficult to restrain myself from running around and around the table, yelling, "Look at this! How do you like that? Wotta spread!" But, I contained myself and to the compliments, I murmured my "thank- you" as graciously as I could.

Ghulam had excelled himself, and the table was laden buffet-style with a variety of the most beautifully prepared food. He had catered to the Hindus, the Mohammedans and to the Europeans. Decorating the table were bowls filled with floating gardenias. Wine sparkled in glasses. Among the roast chickens, salads and savories were curry dishes and plates of Indian sweets. Baskets of popadums, looked like massive, golden-brown potato chips. He had made sausage rolls to melt in your mouth, and spicy hot samosas, triangular shaped pastries filled with spiced meat. Nothing was forgotten. Mike and I took him off to one side in the shadows, complimented him, and gave him a well-deserved reward. We sat at the tables with our ice cream and fruit, while the servants served trays of coffee and liqueurs and a triumphant Ghulam directed operations.

The next morning, everything was in order. The smiling servants had their baksheesh tucked in their pockets. The bigger a party a Sahib holds, the more boasting his servants do. Mike and I went up several notches in their estimation, supplying them with months of conversation with other cooks and bearers.

11

life in the bungalow

THE CLANGING OF KEROSENE oil tins told me that Gajada was putting in our baths. Dukharan was there, busily bossing him about while he arranged the bath mat, towels and soap. Picking up the *Statesman*, I wandered into my bathroom in a dream. I spread the paper on the floor and sat down on my thunder box. Bending over, I began idly turning the pages and giggling at the ads for brides. One in particular caught my eye, "wanted for a fair educated Shrivastana boy (failed BA) a bride of similar caste, age 15. A virgin, (or almost a virgin)."

Someone entered my dressing room. Feeling sure it was Mike, I went on reading. The door behind me opened. Without straightening up, I turned my head to ask why he hadn't knocked. The words froze on my lips. There stood Dukharan. Keeping the same position, I stared back at him. He suddenly vanished, leaving only a swaying curtain. I was embarrassed! I had never been so embarrassed! Blushing furiously, I sat miserably in my bath planning what to do or say when next I came face to face with him.

"Don't be silly," I told myself, "it won't be the first bottom Dukharan's seen!" Everywhere you looked in India, you saw bottoms. But then I thought, they were brown, and it was different somehow. The brown ones weren't so stark. But face him I must, so hurriedly dressing, I went into the drawing room and pressed the bell. Dukharan, with an inscrutable face, entered. I looked squarely at him and asked for a lemon drink. He returned with the glass, fussed about with the cushions, cigarettes and ash try and left. "There!" I thought, "That wasn't too bad, at least it's over." But I'm willing to bet that for a long time afterwards, whenever

Dukharan thought of the Memsahib, the picture that rose to his mind was of a rather large pink bottom with a startled face peering around it!

I enjoyed the company of many of our Indian friends: the village folk I dearly loved, and the educated Indian, who had travelled widely. But there was a class of English-speaking Indian with whom I was never at ease. I could never squeeze more than a dozen words from them. There they sat, while I desperately searched my mind for a subject of some sort, anything at all to get them talking. I always dreaded seeing them come to call, as it meant an hour of acute embarrassment for me. Mike, if he happened to see them coming, took a dive through the curtains of his dark room and refused to come out, saying in a muffled voice, that he was in the midst of some very delicate work, which he couldn't possibly leave, and so left them to me.

Once, while he hid out in his darkroom, I sat on the veranda with Mr. Prithi Singh, his wife and sister. The women settled themselves down, with half smiles on their faces fastened their eyes upon me, and never uttered a word. I tried Hill Stations, dogs, traveling, and, finally, in desperation, turned to the weather. Mrs. Prithi Singh nodded her head in agreement to everything I said. The sister remained silent, although they could both speak English as well as I. Every so often, they spoke to one another in rapid Hindustani which only helped to embarrass me further, to say nothing of making me angry. All Mr. Prithi Singh could manage in reply to my remarks on the weather was, "When one sees clouds like this—one must expect rain." I longed to throw a bombshell in their midst by coming out with some shocking remark, but could never think of anything. My mind became tired and muddled as it darted madly about picking up and discarding various topics I thought might interest them. So we remained, all staring at one another.

"You needn't say anything." Mike explained to me over and over, whenever I complained of how I felt on these occasions, "They're quite content to just sit." But the habit of keeping the conversation rolling at all costs was too strong within me and I suffered on.

When Mike invited Mr. and Mrs. Bhagat to tea, I dreaded their visit, thinking I was in for another uncomfortable afternoon. Mrs. Bhagat followed a few paces behind her husband with her head lowered and eyes downcast. She and I sat on the lounge and waited for tea. "Whatever could I have in common with her?" I wondered, "Whatever can I talk to her about, our worlds are so far apart." While I felt comfortable with Dukharan's old wife, with Mrs. Bhagat I was speechless. Finally I blurted out that her baby, who had been handed over to a servant to carry about outside, was a sweet child. Actually, I had only seen the back of its head, but happily, I had discovered the key to the problem. To my delight, Mrs. Bhagat started talking and didn't stop the whole afternoon. From the baby's birth, complete with details, through its teething and its numerous bouts of diarrhea (more details) she went on to her several miscarriages, her friends' miscarriages and finally to her mother-in-law!

The old mother-in-law took up at least an hour and she was still complaining about her when I took her to my dressing room to feed her baby. Ignoring the chairs, she sat cross-legged on the floor and launched into a detailed account of her sex life. "This," I thought, "was too good to be true!" All I was expected to do was just sit and listen for a change, and though I wasn't particularly interested in her love life, it was a relief to just sit and say nothing for a change. The ice was broken. Here was another Indian friend I could have. I would learn so many things from her, and I gladly accepted her invitation to tea the following week.

Aziz drove me to her house and Mike promised to come for tea and drive me home. Mrs. Bhagat had asked me for two o'clock and I looked forward to the hours until teatime that I hoped would be full of chatter. I could learn how she lived; we could exchange recipes for curry, and a dozen things I wanted to know. However, a changed woman met me at the door. The reason for the transformation sat in the background: the old Mother-in-law. She closely resembled a horse, had a large mouth crammed with huge uneven teeth and couldn't speak a word of English. Not that I held that against her, I couldn't speak much Hindustani, but it promised to be another difficult afternoon, especially as Mrs. Prithi Singh was also present. So we sat, all staring at one another. If I turned from Mrs. Bhagat and Mrs. Prithi Singh, I met the eyes of the mother-in-law, who would open her mouth and give out with a loud horselaugh and I would giggle nervously back. Then I hurriedly looked away. The other two were still sitting, still staring. Occasionally someone would come out with a bright remark on the colour of my nail polish or the material of my dress, but otherwise I just stared at a vase of hideous artificial flowers standing directly in front of me.

So, the long afternoon wore on and with great relief I heard Mike arrive. Up until then, the attractive Indian greeting of "Namaskar" was new to me. I thought Mike and Henri were just fooling when they greeted one another with palms together as in prayer, bowed in an exaggerated fashion. I didn't know it was like the Western act of hand shaking. So, when Mike greeted the ladies this way, it was with mixed feelings of relief at seeing him, and thinking he was being funny. I outdid Mom-in-law, opened my mouth and screeched a long, loud hysterical laugh! They all turned and looked at me in a startled way. I realized I had committed a faux pas, especially when Mike looked sideways at me and repeated the gesture. All through tea, I tried hard not to giggle. It was only when we were on our way home that I relaxed and we both roared until the tears streamed down our faces.

The next day I received an envelope from the office. It contained a newspaper photo of Lord Louis Mountbatten being presented with a garland by an Indian girl and his hands were together in Namaskar.

"What's good enough for Mountbatten is good enough for your old man!" Mike had written.

Once every few months, we made out an enormous shopping list and took a trip to Allahabad. It was always an exciting occasion. I'd draw money from my account, made out my own list (which I always left behind) and arranged the picnic basket.

Allahabad had real stores, and after months with only the Mirzapur bazaar to shop in, I looked forward to being able to buy make-up, wool, buttons and zippers. The wool very often had moths in it, and some of the shades of Revlon had gone out of fashion long before I had left Vancouver. Although Mike and I seldom quarreled, we always had a good fight in Allahabad. Once when I forgot my money along with my shopping list, we finished our fight before we got to the city.

Bumping along in the station wagon with Aziz fast asleep in the back, we passed the Naini jail and over the bridge that spanned the huge Yamuna River. Away in the distance, I could see the "Sangam" where the Ganges and the Yamuna joined, and where Mahatma Ghandi's ashes had been scattered. We drove up wide streets lined with spreading trees and past sprawling bungalows that boasted beautifully-planned gardens where goats and cows now wandered, eating everything within reach and leaving the flowerbeds ragged and unkempt.

We always made the Indian Coffee house on Canning Road our first stop, as they served the most delicious iced coffee. From there, we made our way to Rama's with the food list. There, unless I kept a tight rein on Mike, he would go completely wild and buy tins and tins of the most expensive delicacies.

"They sure don't trust anyone here," I remarked when I saw that the glass cases holding the goods were heavily chained and padlocked.

With a clerk in attendance, Mike peered into all the shelves while I followed behind watching over his shoulder.

"Pack up a dozen cans of this," he told the clerk.

"Half a dozen," I would say. I watched with amusement as the clerk took a large key ring. After trying all the wrong ones, he finally opened the squeaky doors, took out what we wanted, and carefully padlocked it again. After cutting Mike's order almost in half, I went on to a wool and cloth shop that was owned by two old brothers. I started mulling over the tangled bolts of cloth piled high on the counter and came upon one brother fast asleep beneath. I was used to this habit of his by now, and merely covered him up again, and went on looking. When I had made my choice, I went back, uncovered him, and pulled his big toe. He'd waken and serve me.

In the ribbon and button shop, I bought yards and yards of coloured satin ribbon. I'd never use it all, I knew, and had yards more at home, bought on a previous trip to Allahabad, but there didn't seem to be much else to spend my money on, and it was burning a whopping great hole in my pocket. There were no dress shops, no lingerie other than sari petticoats and no coats or sweaters. So, I bought the ribbon and dozens of cards of buttons. From there, I went to Bata's shoe store to buy a pair of sandals. Here the clerk nearly lost a sale. After discussing various attractive points of the sandal, he exclaimed with great fervor, "All the missionaries wear these. They've got big feet too."

Going out to the dusty street to look for Mike, I stood watching the bicycle rickshaws and ekkas go by. There were a great many Anglo-Indians in Allahabad. Some were coffee-coloured, others pasty white. Nearly all of them wore large topis perched squarely on their heads. The women were dressed in unbecoming short cotton prints. They seemed to be an unhappy band of people who were neither accepted by the Indians or the Europeans. From the little I had learned about them, and the few I had met, I began to understand why. It angered and embarrassed me often to be in the company of English "Memsahibs" and to hear them confide in lowered voices, "but, my dear, she's definitely A-I you know."

"Really? You'd never suspect."

"No, but there's that something, and then if you could see her brother, my dear, he's as dark as my bearer here."

"Really?"

I wondered why they felt this way. What's wrong with being Anglo-Indian, anyway? The few I had met had seemed fairly normal to me. It hadn't entered my head nor did I care, that some were Anglo-Indian, until some kind soul would whisper, "Definitely A-I, you know," as if all Anglo-Indians possessed two heads. To me, that a colour bar existed anywhere in the world was beyond my understanding. For the life of me, I couldn't see why a person with a white skin was any better than a person with a dark one. If they had a mixture of the two, what difference did it make? Gradually I began to realize why they were ridiculed and made the object of so many sly jokes, although the realization didn't make me any less angry over the treatment they received.

While I found it embarrassing to be with Europeans who whispered about them, I found it equally uncomfortable to be with Anglo-Indians who desperately strained to hide the fact they had Indian blood flowing in their veins. Remarks such as, "So I told him straight, you may be able to do that to your Anglo-Indian girls, but you can't do it to me!" made me squirm. It puzzled me, here was a girl who was obviously Anglo-Indian, but who denied it in everything she said. They looked down on the Indian people, who in turn looked down on them. They needlessly reminded one over and over again that they were Greek, Spanish, or even better, Welsh. Their odd sing-song accent resembled the Welsh and not a few of them adopted Wales as their homeland. I longed to meet one, just one, who declared openly that he was Eurasian, and so what? Someone like that I could admire and respect. How dreadful, I thought, to live a life forever on the defensive, alert to the fact that they must always live a lie, and afraid of slights and rebuffs from the two races of people whose fault it was that they existed at all.

I turned into a photographer's shop and found Mike matching wits with the clerk over the prices.

"I have to go down to the bazaar," he told me. "Would you like me to take you to the park where you can eat your lunch in peace?"

I agreed, and after dropping Aziz off to have his lunch, Mike drove me to the park, spread a rug under a shady tree and left me with the picnic basket. I relaxed with my back to the tree until I discovered a large black cow eyeing me. Fixing me with its huge eyes, it started toward me. With a chicken leg in one hand and a sandwich in another, I jumped up, hid behind the tree, and looked nervously around for assistance. Resting by a well, I saw a man and woman watching me curiously and in my best Hindustani, I called out and asked if the cow was all right. They didn't understand, and the cow advanced nearer.

"Was it all right?" I asked again and then their faces lit up.

"Yeh gaya hai, Memsahib, yeh dudh ke waste." It's a cow, it's for milk.

Tired and cranky, we piled into the car and drove through the dusk for home. Oh, how refreshing our baths were! We sat afterwards with our drinks and looked over the newspaper-wrapped parcels. Was it worth it? A few miserable buttons, yards of useless ribbon and boxes of tinned food that the shopper could easily have bought himself. This exhausted feeling, aching in every bone from the bumpy road, eyes sore from the dust and glare—no it wasn't worth it, but a few months would slide by and Mike would say, "How about a trip to Allahabad?" and I would start my list, send to the bank and excitedly plan what to wear.

12

Exodus to the Hills

THE DAYS BECAME unbearably hot. Mahadeo and the other malis waged a continuous battle to keep the lawn green. Our garden became a haven for birds. They fell to the grass and lay with wings outstretched; beaks open as they gasped for air. There they stayed, until revived by the cool water being pumped from the well through stone irrigation channels and out onto the lawn. The brain fever bird started its shrill call and as the days grew hotter, so its cry grew louder and more frantic.

Early every morning, the doors and windows were shut and the shutters closed against the heat. I found it most depressing, living in a darkened bungalow all day with the fans going full blast, but only managing to stir up the heavy, stuffy air. Dust storms came, and the grit sifted through every crack to lie deep upon everything in the house and to get into our eyes, mouth and hair. Mike thrived through it all and seemed oblivious to the discomfort, saying,

"What would you do if you were here when it gets really hot? 117 and 118 degrees!"

"118 degrees? Could it get any hotter?" I asked, pushing the damp hair from my forehead.

Natalie hadn't been feeling well, so down to the Mission she went one afternoon to see Evelyn. "Around November 11th," Evelyn told her. So, Natalie and I, already great friends, had another thing in common. Elaine told us of a nice boarding house in Mussoorie, and Mike arranged for us to stay there. We had been warned that it was fatal to go away to the same hill station. It never works out, we were told. You can't bear the sight of each other when you return. But Natalie and I had more faith in our friendship and not only decided on the same hill station, but to share the same rooms.

I couldn't put any enthusiasm into my packing. I wanted nothing whatever to do with the warm skirts and sweaters that lay ready to be put into my suitcase. Lying in my stuffy dim bedroom while the fan laboured overhead, I would try to visualize Vancouver in April. A cool wind would be blowing from the snow on the mountains. The stores would be dressed for spring and shivering people would be gazing longingly at the shop windows with their displays of cotton dresses and beach outfits. They could look at them, even buy, them but wouldn't wear them for some time to come. Other days the city would be under low clouds and people would be hurrying along through a grey rain.

What I wouldn't give, I thought, for a few drops of Vancouver's cool, cool rain right now! I lost myself in visions of children racing to the park with baseball bats, the first sign that spring was well and truly on her way. "Yo-Yos" and marbles would make their appearance and girls would be sitting in the school grounds playing jacks. Crocuses and Hyacinths would be well up by now, I thought. Our so recently beautiful garden was now dry and brown. Dust devils continuously swirled up the paths and over the empty flowerbeds. Only a short time before, the orange, lemon and lime trees stood laden with fruit. Now Mahadeo had to search for the odd orange for our breakfast. Vegetables had disappeared, except for the Indian corn and leeks that, by now, I was very tired of.

Except for being separated from Mike, I looked forward to Mussoorie. I wanted to see this other side of India, her hill stations. All my life I had been fascinated by the Himalayas and pored over books and photos of those tremendous mountains. I followed every expedition to Mount Everest. Although we should only be in the foothills, the ranges of snow-capped mountain, so I had read, were often to be clearly seen in the distance. The old hill station life of the "Memsahib" didn't appeal to me, and anyway, that had disappeared in this new India.

Mussoorie, Simla, Niaini Tal and Darjeeling, no longer played host to hundreds of Army "hot weather" widows who wiled away the time attending bridge, cocktail, and dinner parties. Mike told me of the days preceding the war when he had visited such places, and had been asked,

"What regiment are you with, Mr. Norbury?"

"None," Mike answered. "I'm a carpet manufacturer."

"Trade?" They asked in shocked voices. "Really?" Whereupon, he was instantly dismissed.

Dukharan, who was coming with us to help on the journey, supervised my packing and fussed like an old Granny.

"He wants me to take a walking stick," I told Mike.

The very thought of it appalled me. I knew I was rather large, but a walking stick! But he wouldn't take no for an answer and the walking stick was slipped into my bedding roll. Dukharan dug out my raincoat. I hadn't thought of it, but it, too, was packed along with a lot of other things I had discarded. I found later that he was perfectly right, I should have taken all the wrong things if it hadn't been for Dukharan.

The day to leave came at last. Everyone crowded around to see us away and send us off with the happiest wish they felt they could offer, that I would bring back a son. In the cool of the morning, we picked up Natalie, and laden with luggage, we settled ourselves down for the long uncomfortable trip to Allahabad. The sun was well up when we drove into the station where we got out to stretch and ease our cramped and aching limbs.

Mike, with a camera, binoculars, a thermos of water and baskets hanging every which way from his shoulders, barged up the platform with two pale grubby looking Memsahibs trailing along in his wake. Porters, balancing huge piles of luggage upon their heads, called for the way to be made clear, but no one paid the slightest attention to them. Men with large tin milk cans wandered by calling "ice cream, ice cream." Some sold pan and others peanuts, calling out in long drawn out voices, "Momphalli, Bad am, Momphalli Bad Am." Natalie and I stopped the toy and magazine peddler. We each bought a pile of detective stories, and armed with our magazines, bags of peanuts and our faithful picnic basket, we climbed aboard. Mike paid off the coolies and joined us in the compartment. Dukharan fussed about making things as comfortable as possible, and then with a last look about and a worried glance at me, he left for the section of the train where he was to ride. Soon the dining car bearer appeared for Mike's large order of curry and tea and after a few flags were waved, the train slid silently out of the station.

The sun that had been beating down upon the train all morning turned it into a furnace. Even my magazines failed to take my mind off the heat, so that when we stopped at the next station, Mike bought tin trays filled with blocks of ice and trained the fans on them. It did bring relief, but only for a few miles. Natalie and I even rested our feet on them but the ice quickly melted and the floor of the compartment was filled with dirty water that slopped about as the train swayed along.

At every station, Mike filled the doorway with his bulk and Natalie and I glared through the windows, but it didn't stop a pleasant looking Kashmiri couple from coming in to share our compartment for the rest of the day. They sat in one corner of the long leather seat and stared at us. They stared for miles and miles, past station after station and finally they arrived at their destination and rose to leave, but not before they had informed us that they had a son, "six feet tall, with bright red hair and freckles." I managed to smile weakly.

Natalie murmured, "Really?"

And Mike muttered, "Jolly good show!" and they left.

Throughout the long, hot night, I tossed and turned on the narrow berth. Dukharan had made up our beds beautifully, but mine was now a tangled lump and I was so dirty. The train roared on and through my mind ran the words I had so often read in the *Statesman*,—"and then the train rolled down the embankment." I lay and held my breath as it ran over bridges and rounded curves at what seemed an excessive speed.

The heat must make me worry so, I thought. Why, all of a sudden, should I be so afraid for myself? Why should I have visions of train wrecks and dreadful scenes of havoc when on any other of my many trips, thoughts such as these had never entered my mind? Then "Peanuts" gave me a violent kick. I realized, with a sudden shock and a rush of tenderness, that it was because of her I had become so worried. There wasn't only myself to take care of now, but Peanuts as well. I lay wondering what she was like: fair curly hair and blue eyes, I hoped. I fell asleep.

Early the next morning, we were up making tea on our faithful "Beatrice." The rickety kerosene burner accompanied us on all our journeys.

I secretly felt that Mike would far rather leave me behind than "old Beat." She was always packed in a basket along with the inevitable bottle of Dettol and the carbolic soap. I used gallons of Dettol on journeys in India, especially to clean out the washbasin in the bathrooms as we suspected the basin was used for reasons other than washing. Dukharan came in, and in his quick, efficient manner, tidied up our compartment before disappearing back to his own unbelievably crowded car. I stood swaying in the tiny bathroom scrubbing myself with carbolic soap until I stung. Long tidemarks ran up my arms, my eyes were red-rimmed from lack of sleep and my hair had escaped to hang in greasy lank strands. Putting on a fresh dress, I joined Mike and Natalie. We sat sipping our tea and watched the strange countryside slide by.

The villages seemed cleaner and neater than those at home. The houses were sturdier and the people who came to wave at the train appeared happier and more carefree. We pulled into Dehra Dun and Natalie and I stood well to one side of the platform while Mike and Dukharan saw to the luggage. There were other groups of Europeans gathering up their bags, dressed in cotton dresses and topis. They were obviously missionaries bound for Mussoorie and Landour, where many of them would attend language school.

"Just think, Natalie," I remarked thoughtfully, "this is going on all over India, this grand exodus to the hills—what it must have been like a few years ago with the British Army here. This station must have been one of many just jam-packed with wives and families."

Now when one spotted a European, you gazed curiously, trying to figure out what they were doing in India. Soldiers of the Indian Army strode by, neat and polished in their smart green uniforms. They wore their uniforms proudly and there wasn't a sloppy man among them.

With the crowd we streamed through the gates to where cars, ekkas, tongas and buses waited. In the midst of all the confusion, we were settled in the back of a large long car, waiting for our bags to appear. The windows of the car and the glass partition were of pale, mauve purdah glass. It enabled Muslim women in purdah to watch the people outside without anyone being able to see them. We wound down the windows and watched the coolies sorting the baggage. Leprous beggars swarmed around us. One with his nose eaten away, and stumps for arms, thrust his head in the window. "Baksheesh, Memsahib, salaam Memsahib," he whined and the car was full of flies. Women pushed half-starved babies up to the window. "Hamara Baba bukh lagta hai," they sobbed. It was a relief to be on our way.

As the plains fell quickly behind us, Natalie and I excitedly chatted and bounced about in our seats as the scenery changed and strange new flowers and trees came into view.

"Look behind, Mary. See how far away the plains are now."

"Look, Nats. Look how they plant their crops in steps up the sides of the hills."

"Quickly, this side. There's a whole family of monkeys."

The road became steeper, more narrow and to us suddenly terrifying. The driver drove with careless abandon. Hanging his head out of the window, he followed the white line painted on the road. We twisted and turned to the tune of grinding gears and squealing brakes. The scenery no longer held our interest. Natalie was a delicate shade of green and so was I, she informed me. Mike, who was thoroughly enjoying the ride, slid back the partition and insisted upon pointing out various things he thought would interest us.

"See the giant cactus, and notice the attractive way the hill people dress? I say, you both look a bit queer. Are you alright?"

I shook my head and puffed up my cheeks. He quietly slid back the glass and left us to our misery. Would the journey never end? It took two hours and Natalie just made it out of the car. I held her head over the side. Forever after that, it was always pointed out to the family and friends, "Look dears, there's where Auntie Natalie was ill on her first trip up!"

We climbed into rickshaws, great heavy vehicles with two men pulling and three pushing. We came to a flat stretch of road and were soon sailing along at top speed while the coolies' bare feet made rhythmic slapping sounds on the pavement.

Overlooking deep valleys, the road wound around the sides of hills thick with Rhododendrons, bushes, and plants we had never seen before. We passed large white houses that clung to the sides of the hills as if at any minute they would let go and crash into the valley below. As it was fairly early in the season, the houses had a sad air about them. Very few were occupied. Some had boarded windows and "for sale" signs outside them.

Mike called out from his rickshaw behind, "Look, across the valley, the snows!" We stared entranced, range after range of snow capped mountains lay in the distance.

"The Himalayas! Natalie, can you really believe we're here?"

The panting coolies strained to a stop at the entrance to a beautifully cool-looking garden. We could see "Hillcrest House," a large, white, gracious-looking home covered with Wisteria. This was a house that promised to be full of exciting passageways and attractive verandas. The house was built on a narrow spit of land. The ground fell steeply off on either side into deep valleys.

As we struggled up the driveway, a very old lady on the arm of her ayah met us. "Welcome!" she said, in a thin quavering voice. "What mission are you from?"

"None," replied Mike. "I am a carpet manufacturer."

Cupping her hand to her ear she screeched, "Which mission did you say?"

"None," he hollered. "I'm a carpet manufacturer from Mirzapur."

"Oh well, welcome anyway. My housekeeper, Mrs. Felker, will show you to your rooms." Leaning heavily upon her ayah's arm, she tottered on.

Her name, we found, was Miss Teddingwell. Hillcrest House had been her home since girlhood and she had turned it into a rest home for missionaries. We felt she would never quite forgive us for being in the carpet trade, especially as we found later that Miss Teddingwell boasted of living a life of "sinless perfection" during the past seven years. What she had done during the previous eighty was anyone's guess. As we entered the broad veranda, Mrs. Felker came bustling out. Stout, jolly and with merry eyes, she ushered us into our suite, promised to order our baths, and then took Natalie upstairs to a room she would occupy until Mike returned home in a few days.

The coolies streamed in with the luggage. Dukharan began to unpack, and I explored what was to be our home for the next three months. Leading off the large bedroom was a cozy sunroom. I knelt on the padded window seat, and opened the windows wide onto a secluded part of the garden. Dukharan came in silently. He squatted down, removed my shoes, and put on slippers. "Gussel tayair hai Memsahib," he said and I thankfully went in to have my bath. Once again, I blessed him. Dresser drawers were filled with fresh clothes. Suits and coats were hung away and shoes lay in neat rows.

"You've done well," Mike told him. Handing him some money, he sent him away for food and told him that he was free until next morning.

"I don't want to be disturbed for half an hour," I informed Mike as I closed the door. "I'm going to lie and soak."

The bathroom was dark like every other bathroom found in buildings like Hillcrest House. So, I inspected each corner before closing the outside doors: the old chipped enamel chamber pot with a lid that didn't fit, a brown thunder box with drunken looking iron legs, and, of course, the round tin tub.

I slipped off my clothes and stood looking at the bath. It was rather the same shape as I was these days, and I lowered myself gingerly into it. Nearly all the water rose to the top and a considerable amount spilled over the side. With my legs doubled up and pressed close to my tummy, my knees well up near my chin. I fished around, found a space by my feet, and started to wash. I had just finished my face and neck when the soap shot out of my hand across the room. When I tried to get out to retrieve it, I found to my horror I was firmly lodged and couldn't find anything to pull on! I sat and reviewed the situation. I could hear Mike splashing happily in his tub next door, and I knew if I called him, I should never live it down. So, I grasped the sides of the tub, rocked gently to and fro, and finally lunged out. I firmly resolved to bathe kneeling down in the future.

After a large breakfast, we decided to stroll over to the hospital to make ourselves known. We thought would, at the same time, walk around Mussoorie and Landour and be back well in time for lunch. "The Community Hospital?" Mrs. Felker asked, "Well, you will first have to pick up rickshaws outside the hotel farther up, and ride to the Tibetan shops in the Landour bazaar. At that point, the path is too steep for rickshaws, so you change to dandys. Shall I pack you a lunch?"

"But how far is the hospital from here? Can't we walk?"

"In your condition? I should say not! It's about eight miles and uphill nearly all the way!"

We hailed rickshaws and set out. In the beginning, the road was level until we came to the Kuluri bazaar. Nats and I found ourselves tilted up on our seats gazing down at a hill that fell steeply away below us. A cloth shop stood at the extreme end. From there, the road veered sharply off to the right and disappeared around a corner.

"Let's get out!"

"It's too late, we've started!"

Grabbing one another with one hand and the sides of the rickshaw with the other, we sat in horrified silence as the coolies strained to hold the rickshaw under control. The men in front leaned back and seemed almost parallel to the ground as they turned the rickshaw over to one side of the road, hesitated, then swung sharply over to the opposite side! Zig-zagging over the cobblestones, we inched our way down the dreadful hill. Sweat poured down the coolies' foreheads and ran down to drip off their noses. Splayed feet gripped the road and the muscles in the backs of their legs knotted and bulged. The shop drew nearer. Surely we would crash right on through it, when a sudden order from a man in front, a grunted reply from behind, and up went the front of the rickshaw and we took the corner at full speed, sailing past the shop and on up the road! People fell over one another getting out of our way and the coolies shouted warnings as we flew along. People yelled, cursed, and finally burst into laughter at the sight of two pale looking Memsahibs holding on like grim death with their eyes tightly shut! The pace slackened, we opened our eyes and found before us a long winding hill. Stopping the men, we climbed out to walk, while the coolies plodded on behind.

Near the clock tower at the top of the hill, we sat in the rickshaw again and jogged through the Landour bazaar. Through narrow winding streets we rode, while the coolies again called aloud their warning and dodged crowds of men, women, children, and dogs. Indian music poured forth from the open-faced shops that lined the street. Jewelry, cloth, shoes, toys, fruit, vegetables, and sweet shops with baskets piled high with sticky sweets sat poised over the foul smelling open drains running below. Young Sikh boys in colourful turbans wrestled and played in the doorways of tailor shops. Groups of men sat gambling, many lay asleep amidst the confusion while barbers sat calmly by the roadside trimming hair as well as shaving their customers' underarms.

Pulling to one side by the Tibetan shops, we waited while Mike paid the coolies. A religious procession wound by thumping drums, clashing cymbals and weird chanting mingled with the thousands of other sounds filling the air around us. We sat watching a wonderful old man turning his prayer wheel, while Tibetan women in their multi-coloured aprons beamed at us. The perfect little coffee-hued babies, slung on their backs, peeked shyly over their mothers' shoulder. Here the dingy shops were crammed with attractive beaten silver jewelry: heavy anklets, nose rings, earrings, necklaces and bracelets, as well as oddly shaped boxes studded with turquoise and amber.

Reluctantly, we turned away. Down the hill running, slipping, and sliding came a crowd of men bearing wooden boat-shaped "Dandys." They shouted, pushed, and shoved one another. They were all talking at once, while Mike chose the two dandys we would hire. Natalie climbed into hers and was borne cheerfully away up a path as steep as the side of a house, while my coolies looked at me and promptly demanded double fare.

Refusing to submit to the indignity of being carried, Mike walked along by my side and we pushed on upward. We passed what I remarked were rather odd-looking horses until Mike condescendingly informed me they were mules. They wore heavy turquoise coloured beads around their necks and bells tinkled merrily as they trotted by.

Higher and higher, we climbed. I looked down beyond the Sawalik hills at the plains in varying shades of mauve and purple lying in the distance. We finally turned up a path past a sign that read "Landour Community Hospital." I was gently lowered to the ground outside its doors.

Dr. Fleming was an American, tall and motherly looking. She wore her lovely grey hair piled high upon her head. After our examination, and with an appointment to appear in two weeks, we again climbed into the dandys and set off to find Dorothy, who, we discovered, was living atop the highest hills surrounding the hospital. Dorothy loved her missionary life and had quickly learned a fair amount of Hindustani. She was longing for the day when she could be away to start her work among the people on the borders of Nepal.

We sat drinking tea and talking of our journey on the "Silver Spray," but the two rather staid looking Canadian girls living with her rather cramped our style, so we kept to the zoos we had seen and the fun we'd had in the ship's pool. Of the dance halls and bars we had visited we kept silent, for although Dorothy had never touched any drink stronger than lemonade, and had always behaved in a manner befitting a missionary, I felt that memories of our night life were better left out.

The morning Mike was to leave for home, I awoke with a lost feeling. "How strange it will be without him," I thought. Countless times I turned to him for help with the language and customs I didn't understand. There were so many things I hadn't bothered to learn. If I took a rickshaw, what did I pay? How did one tell the man to stop, go slowly, or wait ten minutes, and how much should I tip? I had no idea of the value of Indian money, and now for the next few months there would be no more signing of chits to be sent to the office for payment. Letters wouldn't be whisked mysteriously away and mailed, and there would be no Dukharan to fuss over me. Small things, all of them, but suddenly magnified as I watched Dukharan give my room a last flick with his duster, sling the thermos over his shoulder, and turn to salaam me "Goodbye." As he disappeared out of the door, Mike and I sat on the edge of the bed.

"You have your bank account, but if you run short, wire for more. I've left you stacks of writing paper and stamps and shall write every day. Take good care of yourself, darling, and remember if you need me, I can be here in twenty four hours. Otherwise, I shall be up in July."

We said goodbye and I watched his rickshaw jog out of sight. Natalie and I had now joined the army of hill station "Widows" we had so often read about.

13

Missionaries

GRADUALLY "HILLCREST HOUSE" filled with tired-looking missionaries, weary from their journey in third class carriages. Their joy to be up in the cool hills with a few weeks' rest before them was almost pitiful. Many had been to "Hillcrest House" before, some from years back, and Natalie and I sat silently through each meal listening to them reminisce of past years, and inquire over and over again, "Is 'Miss So and So' coming again this year?" "Will 'Reverend Whatnot' be up?" We found, also that after they had determined just who was arriving again, the conversation always turned to two things, from the main course right thru to coffee. Firstly, which was the more hair-raising road, the "Naini Tal" or the "Dehra Dun" to Mussoorie, and secondly, the difference in size and price of hill eggs in comparison to eggs on the plains.

Natalie and I, suddenly thrust into this life, both felt it all unreal. It was rather as if we were watching a play, but having no part in it whatsoever. However, we envied these people their casual way of shrugging off numerous hot weathers spent on the plains and their beautiful Hindustani.

Across from us sat a woman who didn't quite fit into the group. Her name was Mrs. Wilmot from Cawnpore. As her husband travelled about India a great deal, she had come to her birthplace, Mussoorie, for a holiday. Smartly dressed in lovely English skirts and Liberty scarves, she was often a perfect dinner companion. Her knowledge of Mussoorie in the by-gone days was abundant, and we plied her with questions. Often though, she would dash in late for dinner, lipstick smudged, hair hanging limply and there she sat, not saying a word and looking more depressed by the minute. She fiddled. She fiddled with her hair, her pearls and finally with the cutlery before her. Natalie and I stared in fascination as she fiddled knives, forks, spoons, salt and pepper about until they rested before the person by her side. Her unfortunate dinner companion then sat with her head lowered, looking in a bewildered fashion at all the articles she had mysteriously acquired. We sat and held our breath as the bearer hovered over Mrs. Wilmot with the serving dishes, waiting patiently while she and her partner sorted out the plates, knives and forks. Mrs. Wilmot nodding, giggling, thanking and apologizing until everything was arranged and she had helped herself to the first course. She was a rapid eater, so by the time the sweet course was on its way, the whole thing was re-enacted.

"It must be her nerves," Natalie and I concluded, "she must miss her husband terribly, poor thing, and I don't think she is too used to the company of missionaries."

One evening we invited Mrs. Wilmot to our rooms for a drink before dinner. She was in delightful form and while we were laughing over an amusing story she had just told us, the gong rang for dinner. Mrs. Wilmot shot up out of her chair and without another word to us, flung open the window of our little sitting room and with one graceful leap disappeared out into the night. Natalie and I stared at one another.

"Wherever has she gone?"

"Can't you guess?"

"Of course. She must drink. Why ever didn't we catch on before?"

Sure enough, Mrs. Wilmot breezed in during the soup course completely "sozzeled." To take a dozen or so faithful missionaries who had most surely signed the pledge years before and what's more kept it, and throw a Mrs. Wilmot amongst them, will if nothing else, take the conversation away from eggs.

Leaning across the table, her voice now hoarse and loud, Mrs. Wilmot yelled—"You were asking me about Mussoorie in the old days. Well, all I can say is that the ghosts must look down now and have a good laugh. You know that hotel up the road?" We said we had noticed it and she went on,

"Well—that, believe it or not, used to have a bachelor's ringing-out bell."

"A what?"

"A bachelor's ringing-out bell. You see, the station was crammed with Army wives and every morning at about 6 o'clock the bell rang for all the bachelors to go back to their own rooms in time for early morning tea."

Natalie and I felt that this discussion could very well have been carried on in the seclusion of the garden the following morning. There we could have asked all the questions that were burning in our minds. But not here, definitely not here.

"Is Reverend Winthrop coming again this year?" one lady bravely broke in to ask. Before Mrs. Felker could answer, the voice of Mrs. Wilmot boomed out again.

"Yes, the wildest hill station it was then, and look at it now. What do you see going on in that hotel these days? Canasta parties and knitting. The only bit of fun you see there now is an ayah having her bottom pinched by a hotel bearer behind the bushes."

Dead silence. Natalie and I desperately strived to change the conversation. By then, Mrs. Wilmot was engaged in retrieving her cutlery and eating her sweets. Then, over coffee, and through clouds of smoke she quoted, "O, moon of my Delight, that knowest no wane!" and made rude remarks in French to the Padres.

Natalie and I settled down to our knitting and waiting. Every few weeks we were notified that money had been deposited to our accounts, upon which news we flew to the bank and spent a few days on a wonderful shopping spree. We spent hours in Sahib Singh's chemist shop mulling over the latest make-up and taking an age to buy a lipstick. We took rickshaws to the Kulri bazaar, careful now to get out at the top of the hill and walk down. The clerks lounging in the doorways of their shops rushed out and followed us along the street beseeching us to buy. At first we politely told them no, and often stopped to tell them that we weren't looking for whatever they had to offer. But we soon caught on, continued chatting to one another, and ignored them. There were two kinds of shopkeepers, one dozed in the corner and ignored us while the other's idea of salesmanship was to be as insistent as possible. We set out to buy some wool.

"No, we have no P & B ply blue, madam, but would you be interested in buying a fly flap or a pair of sunglasses?"

"No thanks, I just want the wool."

"Oh! Just a moment," and diving behind the counter, poking and rummaging about, he arose with a tottering pile of boxes.

"See? Only yesterday, I received from my shop in Delhi, this beautiful set of hair grips. Here is some of the latest scent," and taking off the screw top, he waved a bottle of violent smelling toilet water under our noses. Natalie and I edged toward the door—"Sorry, you haven't got what we're looking for"—and we turned to go.

"Knitting needles? Safety pin? Combs? Material? Lovely material." and by this time his voice rising hysterically, he desperately pulled out bolts of cloth and grabbing anything within reach, he waved various articles madly about in the air as he followed us out into the street. In another shop, dealing exclusively in wool, the sleepy clerk displayed everything from fiery orange 4 ply to deep purple 2 ply and then after one of us spotted a brand new box of P & B 3 ply, he reluctantly wrapped it up and took our money.

Every two weeks we trekked to the hospital. Although Natalie's appointments were just once a month, she always faithfully accompanied me. Leaving immediately after breakfast, we rickshawed to the Kulri, paid off the men, and walked the remainder of the way. It was a good day's journey for us, the steep hills we laboriously plodded up and down, the long wait to see the doctor and the window-shopping we never could resist. The one bright spot was the "Kwality" ice cream shop where we stopped for a treat on our way back. The "Kwality" perched on the side of the hill. They served sandwiches and ice cream sundaes American style. Outside on a gravel covered piece of ground surrounded by a tired garden, stood umbrella shelter tables where, as you sat devouring their rich concoctions, there lay before you an unparalleled view of the plains. This was the "point of no return" on our walk back from the hospital. Once the Tibetan shops and long winding hill was behind us, it made the homeward trek somehow shorter as we planned what to order. One especially hot day we rested half way up the Kulri hill and held a serious discussion.

"Have you decided yet, Mary?"

"I think I'll have a strawberry sundae."

"But we had that last week."

"So we did. Pistachio?"

"No, let's try the pineapple. Come on, Mary."

Spurred on by visions of our sundae, we quickened our pace and arrived hot and tired at the "Kwality" to sink gratefully in the chairs outside. Our sundaes sat invitingly before us: ice cream, chunks of juicy pineapple topped with whipped cream and walnuts. We waited, savouring the moment. It was a moment worth remembering like a hot bath at the end of a long journey or the first drink at sundown. Reverently we took up our spoons when a movement caught my eye. Amongst the whipped cream and walnuts atop my beautiful sundae squirmed a horrible large, fat, orange insect. Aghast, my whole day ruined, I called the bearer and with a trembling finger, pointed. The waiter laughed. He actually laughed, and then taking up the glass, he dug his fingers into the whipped cream, removed the insect, placed the sundae before me again and knocked four annas from my bill!

Every morning after breakfast, we crossed the hall into the drawing room for prayers. This room had every conceivable dust catcher in all Asia. Jutting out over the pokey little fireplace was a massive mantelpiece that held countless ivory carved figures resting on crocheted doilies. Above this, a dark wooden affair of latticework climbed up the wall. Leaves, roses and vines twisted in and out and it, overpowering everything in the room. I felt my eyes irresistibly drawn to this monstrosity. I wondered who the person had been, years and years ago, who'd thought it beautiful and had dared have the "Thing," (as my mind labelled it) packed up the mountain on the back of some perspiring coolie.

Large brass pots contained aspidistras and artificial flowers. Every overstuffed chair and settee was strewn with lacy antimacassars. It was not unusual to see a lady leave the room at a dignified stroll, knitting under one arm, Bible under the other, with a lace "doo-dad" dangling from her "bun." Small collapsing Kashmiri tables stood throughout the entire room. On their brass tops precariously balanced ivory elephants, china vases, and metal elephant bells. One knock set the whole collection flying from one table to another until two or three of them lay scattered on the faded, rose-patterned carpet.

Miss Teddingwell took her meals alone, and was already enthroned in her special chair when we filed into the room. With one hand grasping her cane and a large worn Bible resting on her lap, she peered over her spectacles, and greeted each one in turn. As she was deaf, the conversation veered from normal tones to loud shouts.

"Good morning, Miss Teddingwell. I enjoyed my breakfast, I must say these hill eggs are a joy after the small ones on the plains."

"Good morning, my dear, what were you saying?"

"Eggs, Miss Teddingwell, I was telling Miss Johnston that the eggs here are much bigger."

"Legs? Whose legs are bigger?"

"EGGS, MISS TEDDINGWELL!"

"It's the climbing. You're not used to it after the plains. That's what does it."

"EGGS, MISS TEDDINGWELL!"

"Oh yes, but you'll get used to it after awhile," and she turned away. Her expression plainly showing that legs weren't quite the things to converse about at any time, especially just before prayers.

As Natalie and I became larger, the sessions grew longer. We had the greatest difficulty in keeping still, especially when a tickling sensation crawled from my toes up my legs and into my back. Being unable to stand it, I'd give a violent jump. To relieve it, I had to have my spine massaged. Natalie's hand would steal around to my back and gently knead it with her fingers.

May and June passed by, and the mound of matinee jackets and booties rose higher. We merrily knitted away under the Deodar trees, in bed after early morning tea, or in the drawing room after dinner. Our journeys to the hospital were weekly now and took less time. We grew accustomed to the hills.

The coming of the mailman was the highlight of each day. We clustered around Mrs. Felker as she sorted out the stacks of letters and magazines on the veranda.

"Mrs. Stirner, nice lot for you today. Mrs. Quakenbuah, two for you—Natalie, one from your husband and some magazines from Scotland. Mary, your usual from Mike. One from Canada and some magazines."

Taking our mail, we retired to the garden. Except for the rustling of paper, there was silence as each of us read our letters. Every piece of news was hungrily absorbed. Our mothers were sending parcels. Friends were having babies. Neighbours sent their love. After exchanging news, we unwrapped our fat rolls of magazines and enviously studied the slim models posed in the latest fashions from London, Paris and New York. We often fell into fits of giggles as we looked at each other's ungainly figures and down at our sloppy sandals.

Next to the mailman, we looked forward to our meals and clock-watched for fully an hour before each one. Half an hour before dinner, we washed and changed into the same old outfits: Natalie in a blue and white cotton crossover dress and me in a voluminous navy blue two-piece. We brushed our hair, put on a dash of lipstick, no time for mascara these days as there was that sleeve to finish before dinner. And so we sat, perched on the edge of our beds knitting, ears alert for the first stroke of the gong, ready to rush out. Often we thought we heard the bell, and would dash headlong into the hall to fall over an amazed Akbar as he prepared to beat the gong and parade through the hallways. Red with embarrassment, we would fiddle with the potted plants arranged throughout the hall, all the time sidling towards the dining room and as Akbar turned the corner at the end of the passage. If the gong was late in sounding, everyone congregated on the veranda and sat glancing at their watches with worried frowns on their faces. Natalie and I were past masters at reaching the table first and were always standing ready behind our chairs for Grace as the others filed in.

We were playing a game of guessing what was for dinner. It made little difference that it was nearly always mutton, boiled potatoes and green beans. Occasionally, the potatoes were roasted and once we had chicken. Apart from that, there was the sweet to consider: something nice and filling like a suet pudding was always welcomed with signs of approval. The dessert that caused the greatest stir was the Christmas-like pudding served in honour of Miss Teddingwell's 87th birthday. Everyone thoroughly enjoyed it, especially the sauce. We poured ourselves generous helpings. Smacking their lips gently, the ladies asked for the recipe which Mrs. Felker promptly gave them, saying that it was flavoured with "American essence." It wasn't until much later that we discovered the "American essence" was brandy. While the others took it very well, and laughed uproariously, Miss Stubbins became extremely agitated and refused to speak to a soul for the next three days.

My first impression of our fellow lodgers was of pale faces, wispy hair, and rather unattractive dirzi-made dresses. Gradually, as the weeks passed and they emerged as individuals, we acquired a great admiration for them. Miss Blakley, who sat opposite Natalie, seemed a delicate little lady with the most unmanageable hair we had ever seen. She first appeared at the table with her hair neatly combed close to her head. It took less than five minutes for it to rise slowly and stand straight up in the air. There it stayed, waving in the breeze of the conversation around her. Miss Blakley as it turned out, was infinitely stronger and braver than Natalie and me. During dinner one evening, she told us quite casually of a time when she had taken over a bungalow in the Mirzapur district that had stood empty for years.

"It was crawling with kraits," she said.

Natalie and I felt the hair bristling on the backs of our necks.

"Of course, you immediately moved out," we said.

"Of course, I did not!" she retorted. "And there weren't just dozens of the things, but hundreds of them. I'd find them coiled about the chairs, on the veranda, in bathrooms, bedrooms, and on tops of doors. They were everywhere. We massacred kraits for weeks until we found their nests beneath the bungalow and finally cleared them out from there."

"But a bite from a krait kills you less than half an hour, doesn't it? Isn't it one of the deadliest snakes in India?" Natalie and I asked in horrified whispers.

"Yes," she answered. "They're beastly little things."

Miss Blakley ceased to be a defenseless missionary in our eyes and we looked upon her with unconcealed admiration. We pictured her leaping about the shabby bungalow, killing snakes before breakfast, during lunch, and before getting into bed at night while her hair waved defiantly back and forth in the air.

"How wonderful to have no fear of snakes," we breathed.

"But my dears, I'm petrified of them!" she answered.

Beside me at the table sat Miss Snyder. She was immense. Her huge bust hung over the table, interfering with her meals. Miss Snyder's courage took a different form from that of Miss Blakley, but just as daring to us. She regularly, despite her size, rode down the Kulri hill in a single rickshaw! We were convinced that some day she would land slap bang into the middle of the cloth shop at the end of the hill, but she never did. Not that year anyway.

A woman who was often a guest at Sunday dinner was an old friend of Mrs. Felkers'. She owned her own home along by Happy Valley Way. She was rather an awe-inspiring woman of the old school, and a terrific snob as well. Natalie and I avoided her whenever we could. She was frightening in a way, that is, until that dreadful day on the mall. Mrs. Felker and her friend had been shopping. After an ice at the "Kwality," they hailed a rickshaw and climbed in. Mrs. Felker sprawled comfortably back on the seat. Her companion sat straight as a ramrod, adjusting her skirts primly, and putting up her parasol with a flourish. The coolies at the back took up their positions. The men in from bent, grasped the handle, lifted and took off at a fast trot. The shaft parted from the vehicle, and the two men galloped up the road with the shaft, while the rickshaw tipped back on the two men behind. There lay Mrs. Felker and her friend, legs waving in the air and long lace-trimmed knickers in full view of passers by. Mrs. Felker, weak from laughter, turned to watch her companion trying desperately to hold on to her dignity and failing, in such an incongruous position, held tightly to her parasol instead.

The conversation now turned to the rains. Each person knew the date and almost the hour that the monsoon had broken the previous year. We grouped around the old radio and poured over the newspapers.

"The monsoon has reached Calcutta," the all-India radio announcer informed us. "It is moving on to Patna, and Allahabad."

The dust from the dry hot plains rose up 6,000 feet to drift amongst the streets of Mussoorie, and we all felt an air of expectancy.

"118° today," Mike wrote, "I expect the rains by Tuesday."

Natalie and I were awakened from a deep sleep by the thunderous roar of water as it beat down on the corrugated rooftops of the buildings around us.

"The rains, Natalie. Quickly, they've broken!"

We collided in the dark as we rushed about closing windows.

"The light won't work!"

Thunder rolled and cracked around the mountains in deafening roars, weird flashes of lightening lit the room. We stood gripping the old iron bedsteads, white-faced and frightened.

"Any candles?" Nats shouted.

"None." I yelled back.

I was willing to bet that all the other occupants of the house were lighting the candles they'd automatically put by weeks ago, and were calmly closing their windows without any fuss.

"May as well go back to bed," I declared. And we did, in the same bed, with the covers well up over our heads.

A letter from Mike told us the rains had broken in Mirzapur at midnight. He and Chipso rushed madly up and down the lawn, Mike attired only in gumboots and spectacles.

While those in the plains went wild with joy and relief, we in the hills began to shiver. A fire was lit in the drawing room each evening, but Natalie and I more often sat crouched above a little electric heater in our own room. We went to bed early in socks and sweaters and cuddling hot water bottles. Dukharan was right. We seldom moved away from the house without a raincoat and one of those enormous black umbrellas that everyone, including the coolies, carried.

Often we took advantage of a break in the rains to walk along to a spot on the Mall to see the snows. Standing against clear sky, the magnificent ranges loomed up more breath taking than anything we had ever dreamed of. We would stand leaning against the railings watching them change colour: greens, ice blues to soft shades of pink. Finally, thick black clouds rolled before them, blotting them from view and we would hurry back to the house before the rain.

14

Waiting for Judy

"You must come and live in the hospital a few days before your time!" Dr. Fleming told me on my last visit before Mike and David arrived.

"You may not convince the coolies to venture out in the middle of the night because of their fear of panthers. And, too, there's the rain. They usually possess only one outfit, you know. If they get soaked, more often than not, they die very quickly of pneumonia."

I was shown two rooms and chose one that overlooked the plains and the road leading up to the hospital. As Natalie and I walked along the Mall to meet David and Mike, we were suddenly conscious of what three months alone had taught us. We were no longer at a loss for words when the road sweepers asked the time and could carry on a halting conversation with our favourite rickshaw coolies. Shopkeepers, shoe menders and dirzis stopped to pass the time of day. The coolies at the various rickshaw stands gave up rushing wildly to us, dragging their cumbersome vehicles behind them. Instead, they salaamed us cheerfully and went back to dozing or knitting their violently coloured scarves or helmets. We felt a strong sense of belonging and looked forward to the other hot-weathers we would spend here.

We stood by the bandstand waiting for the gate to be opened below, allowing the first cars to come up. The road resembled a long thin snake writhing amongst the hills. As we waited, we heard the first faint blare of horns and a car appeared far below. Then another, until a dozen or more dotted the road looking like tiny black ants. We grew more excited as the noise of the motors came nearer. A coolie, high up on the Mall shouted, "Sahibs ayange! Sahibs ayange!" Without waiting to question how he knew they were our "Sahibs," we hurried down the hill and met David and Mike as they came swinging up the road. As Mike's arms closed around me, I realized how terribly I had missed him. We had so much to say that our words trembled out excitedly as we walked back up to the rickshaws.

Back in our rooms, refreshed after a hot bath, Mike sat with his whiskey and soda telling me the news of Mirzapur. How Chipso had grown, what new fruit trees he had planted and how many new babies there were among the servants. Dukharan had stayed behind, but would be coming up to help on the journey home. The hills during the rains didn't agree with him, making him cold and miserable. The following day, we sat in the Majestic Movie House watching an American show. Leaning close to me in the dark, Mike squeezed my hands and whispered laughingly,

"Do you know, I've just realized, this is the first movie you and I have ever seen together?"

And so it was. There had only been that one date alone before we were married. I whispered back,

"Fancy that, our first movie and here I am all pregnant."

The morning arrived for me to go into the hospital to live, and for Natalie, and David to return home. With my luggage strapped to a coolie's back, we four trekked over to Landour. I checked in at the hospital and walked back to the "Kwality" for an ice cream before saying goodbye to Natalie and David. Back in the hospital, Mike kissed me goodnight and said,

"Only a few more days and 'Peanuts' will be here. We can go home, too. Not long now, darling."

"Not long now" I said to myself on every one of those eighteen days I waited in the hospital on the hill. In the beginning, a procession of Indian nurses trouped in each morning and afternoon to take my temperature and ask in Hindustani, "Any pains yet?" After the first ten days, they continued taking my temperature but discontinued asking how I felt. Instead, they peered at the thermometer, looked at me, and ran giggling from the room. After fifteen days, they even stopped asking my temperature. They just poked their heads around the door and gazed at me with disbelieving looks on their faces. When I was well past the expected date, I ceased to be impatient and settled into a comfortable routine, which I refused to vary. Every morning, I sat in my voluminous nightgown and bed-jacket and knitted.

Knitting became an obsession. I began each pair of socks with the thought that they would never be finished. "Peanuts" was bound to arrive in the middle of making them, and then I should lose all interest. So, I cast on and cast off innumerable pairs of socks until Mike had enough to last for years. I had breakfast by the window. As I ate, I watched for Mike to appear on the path far below. Right in the middle of the meal, a horde of little men came in to clean my room. One cleaned the washbasin in the adjoining bathroom, another the toilet. Others swept, dusted and polished the mirror. I sat with my back to them, as it became embarrassing to greet them each morning. I could tell by their faces that they were beginning to feel I was there under false pretences. Then Mike would appear hurrying around the mountain path. I would grab my knitting and feverishly get in a few rows before he stood below my window and called up

"Still there, darling?"

When he came in the door, I would raise my face for his kiss and bend to my work again. I would have driven another less even-tempered man wild, but Mike, bless him, never once complained although he would have been quite justified in snatching the knitting from my hands and flinging it over the side.

We spent the day together and, after tea, Mike returned to Hillcrest House. Being Mike, he turned up in the oddest outfits. I looked down one morning to find him standing beneath his massive umbrella dressed in shorts (the rather long, English type), a misshapen grey hat lined with spun glass, gumboots, and a war surplus camouflage gas cape he'd bought in the bazaar for 2 rupees. A pale blue and pink striped bag that he used to keep his films dry dangled from his hand.

"Come up quickly." I said crossly, (still knitting). "And don't, for heaven's sake, let on you're mine!"

As he came into the room I grumbled, "Why do you insist on coming to see me in that outfit?"

"Because of the rain," he explained.

"Rain!" I scoffed, "A little rain won't hurt you."

I ate my words the day he persuaded me to drop my knitting and walk to the bazaar. Great torrents of water cascaded down the hillsides and across the paths, to disappear in the drains below. Everything was dripping. Beautiful green ferns grew on every tree. Pink crocuses appeared overnight and the hillside was shrouded in a grey mist. Ahead we could hear a thin piping melody played on a flute, and we came upon a Hillman crouched on the low wall playing contentedly. The plains peeked through the mist below him.

I returned to the hospital clutching a large bag of wool and a new pattern book. I was soaked through to my under things, and my shoes were ruined. Mike, on the other hand, splashed happily through the muddy puddles in the rain. Protected by his gas cape, he kept completely dry.

The half hour before dinner I spent in a room down the hall with Elsie Fenwick, a midwife from Manchester. By some odd twist of fate, she found herself in India as nanny to two small princes. Elsie arrived out in 1947, expecting to be met in Calcutta. Instead, she learned that she was to travel alone to Mussoorie on a train overloaded with refugees. Not understanding one word of Hindustani, and not knowing what she could safely eat and drink, she made her way along through frightening havoc. Screaming and yelling, thousands of misplaced souls fought to board the train as it passed slowly through the stations. Multitudes were living on the platforms.

She arrived in Mussoorie suffering from dysentery that refused to be cured. But in the good old Lancashire spirit, she stayed on to teach and look after the two little boys. For someone who hadn't been much farther from Manchester than Rochdale, the odd customs, intrigue in the Royal household, and difference between her religion and that of her employers must have been most upsetting. But she had come to do a job, and do it she would. She stayed longer than any other nanny the boys had ever had. Her aim was to bring the children safely to an age whereby they could stand one their own feet. She taught them honesty, courage and integrity. At the same time, she tried to be as much like a North Country "mum" as she could be. She knitted their pullovers, mended their clothes and cooked simple meals in a household packed with servants. She treated the Prince and Princess with respect, but she also refused to change from Elsie Fenwick of Manchester. When she spoke to them or of them she called them "Daddy and Mummy." One of the most dangerous snakes in India failed to frighten her. She chased a krait around her cottage with the fire tongs. She wasn't wasting any time calling the Chowkidars. The snake had no business being in the same house as her beloved charges. As it wrapped itself around the table leg, she killed it with one furious blow.

Elsie now lay propped up in her hospital bed recovering from the persistent dysentery and a centipede sting that had brought her close to death. I could follow the path the centipede had taken by the angry looking red marks on one side of her face. From her right cheek, across her eyelid and on to her forehead, the scars appeared like a row of holes left by the tines of a fork. She was recovering rapidly, and we laughed and chatted until dinner time.

"You still here?" Nurse Hardy's plump cheerful face appeared around the door as I was casting on stitches for sock slippers. She was the one and only American nurse on our wing among all the Indian girls. She spoke Hindustani with a strong American accent.

"Still here." I replied. "But when I feel a pain, I shall whistle the Star Spangled Banner!"

Dinner was over, and I had turned out the light for the third time. On the ceiling directly above me hung a large black spider with a cluster of white eggs suspended from its fat tummy. It was disconcerting in the dark not knowing whether she was still there or was preparing to drop onto my face.

"It's the 19th," I thought. "Peanuts is ten days late."

Then I felt a small twinge. Lying still, scarcely daring to move, I held my breath and waited. There it was again! Two hours later, they were stronger. But the tune of the Star Spangle Banner refused to come into my mind, so I put my finger on the bell and held it there.

Nurse Hardy hurried away to find Dr. Ellis, the resident doctor. I had seen Dr. Ellis before this. She was a slim, attractive Indian. I had watched her striding about the hospital making a striking figure in a white coat over her sari, her dark hair coiled about her head. She came silently into the room now in nightie and housecoat, one long gleaming black plait swinging over her shoulder. She bent to examine me, then sent a nurse off to phone Dr. Fleming who lived nearby.

Hours later, as I hung on desperately to the ropes tied by the table, I felt the situation could have been funny, had I not been the centre of attraction. For it appeared that there was a race taking place between an Indian woman in the adjoining room and me. One nurse in particular must have placed heavy bets, for which patient I wasn't certain. But she spent that long, long night clattering from one room to the other in a state of high excitement.

Dr. Fleming, weird in her cap and gown, looked at me with kind eyes above her mask. The matron stood by my side talking quietly. Suddenly there was a clatter from the other room. In popped the gambling nurse to have another look before running madly back. Finally, she appeared with a long sad face. "False labour," she announced. The patient had been wheeled back to her own room and the nurse drooped dejectedly in a corner of the room.

It was growing light outside. The tree frogs set up their usual noisy chatter, and I was asked for the third time if they should put a call through for Mike.

"No, let him sleep. He must have a good breakfast before he sets out."

For weeks I had ignored him and bored him with my interminable knitting. I had ridiculed his clothes and failed to show one ounce of appreciation for the long wet journeys he faithfully took each day. Now, I was suddenly solicitous for him. My pleas were ignored, however, and a nurse was sent to the phone.

I saw Dr. Fleming take up the forceps; someone grabbed my legs and thrust them into stirrups. As I inhaled deeply from the gauze mask, my last thought was of the slippers. I hadn't finished them.

From far away I heard a voice say, "You have a lovely baby girl and she's perfect!" I turned my head to gaze adoringly at little Judith Anne.

The gambling nurse sprang into action with her usual clatter and was soon wheeling me back to my room where Mike waited. The stretcher was easily a foot and a half higher than the bed. I knew then whom she had bet against, for she simply rolled me over like a log before Mike could assist and I dropped onto the bed with a high bounce.

A nurse was ready and waiting at Hillcrest House. When Judy was a week old, I was allowed to leave. Sister Jones was a nurse of the old school. She had my bed ready and warmed with a hot water bottle when we arrived from the hospital. She was horrified at the thought of me up and walking about with Judy only a week old. She insisted that I get right to bed and not even get up to wash. While in the hospital, I had been up since the second day and had done all Judy's woolen washing. In any case, bed bored me. So, I waited until she was back in her own room with Judy before leaping out of bed and locking the door.

I finally got my own way and she turned her full attention to Judy. The next day, as Mike and I rode along the Mall in a rickshaw, I spied a familiar figure dressed in khaki hurrying along the road. It was Dukharan, his face creased by a happy smile. He came over to the rickshaw and touched my hands with his in a way foreign to a Hindu servant.

From the moment Dukharan laid eyes on Judy, he was her slave. It mattered not that it was more befitting a Burrah Sahib to have had a son, Judy Baba was his charge and it was over his dead body that any harm should ever come to her.

Early one morning, we stood watching a band of coolies leave Hillcrest House with our luggage: picnic basket, baby's basket and innumerable other baskets, tin boxes, bedding rolls and ice cream freezer. In a long string, they marched out of the compound with Dukharan in the rear carrying the thermos and wearing an air of great importance. Sister Jones was to accompany us to Dehra Dun. All the way down that hair-raising road, she kept us entertained by pointing out the places she knew of where cars and buses had gone over the side.

As we quickly descended to the plains, we shed our sweaters and took blankets off Judy. Dehra Dun was hot and steamy. Pushing our way through the beggars and porters, we climbed into the privacy of our compartment. The whistle blew and the train slid slowly out of the station. People made mad dashes alongside looking for space. Over their heads, we could see Sister Jones waving a large white handkerchief. The hanky faded from view as the train gathered speed. Mike and I turned to look at one another, not daring to admit that we were both scared stiff. We had never felt so alone in our lives.

Dukharan stayed to make up our beds. He placed Judy's basket away from draughts, adjusted her net, all the time talking to her in a soft soothing voice, with love written all over his face.

How different were the plains now from the dry hot dusty earth I had last seen. Everything was lush and green. We passed buffaloes wallowing contentedly in muddy pools of water. The next day, as we rapidly approached Moghul Sarai Station, the excitement of going home mounted. I felt I couldn't wait to be back in our own bungalow again. Aziz and Sagir were standing by the station wagon grinning broadly. Each was allowed a quick peek at Judy by Dukharan, before he placed her basket in the back of the Morris. We were soon bumping along river-like roads on the twenty odd miles from Moghul Sarsi to Mirzapur.

"Won't it be lovely to be home again?" I asked Mike, as we splashed and skidded about on the muddy road.

"Yes, it's been so long," he answered and then frowned, and bit hard on the end of his cigar.

"What's wrong? What are you thinking about?"

"Molar." grunted Mike, "Molar and his 'Two-bit' band. If he's there waiting for us, I'll be furious. The noise will frighten Judy and upset Chipso and our homecoming will be ruined."

"He won't be," I replied. "Because we're bringing home a daughter instead of a son."

"He'd better not be." Mike warned.

We turned into the civil lines, honked madly as we sailed past Natalie's bungalow, and then swept through our own gates and up the drive. On the veranda, in clean white uniforms, Ghulam and Pir Mohammed waited. Gajada and Suleiman stood holding a wriggling Chipso. In one mad leap, Chipso threw herself at us and then raced round and round the garden clearing high hedges before skidding to a stop. Her lips were drawn back exposing her teeth in a grin. She snuggled into my neck telling me in her own sweet way that she was overjoyed at our all being together again.

Mahadeo shyly presented me with a damp little bouquet of flowers, and Gajada hurried off to fill our baths. The bungalow shone. Covers and curtains were freshly washed and the silver and glass gleamed.

"This is heaven," I thought as I wandered through the bright airy rooms. It was hard to understand why I had been so desperately glad to leave it nearly four months before. The unbearable heat, and the creeping dust were quickly forgotten.

Our large square bedroom had been turned into a nursery for Judy. It was newly painted in pale yellow and robin's egg blue. The Cape Cod doors, over-looking the rose garden were screened, and under the ceiling fan stood a white cot made by Kulu the barrhaee or carpenter. A table held weighing scales and a tiny bathtub. A low nursing chair, an armchair covered in yellow and a glass-fronted wardrobe had been placed in the room. A blue carpet lay rolled in the next room, ready for the cold weather. Pretty yellow and blue curtains hung by the windows and doors.

While I bathed and nursed Judy, Mike made a quick tour of the garden. As he passed the nursery window, I heard him demand,

"Where is Molar?"

"Not here, Sahib," Mahadeo replied.

"And why not?" Mike asked. "He and his band were waiting at the Cros's house when they returned with Alain. It's time he realized that for us a daughter is as precious as a son!" he raved on as they disappeared around the corner of the bungalow.

15

back to the bungalow

NOW WE HAD JUDY, there was one of two things we could do. Look after her ourselves and bring her up in as nearly an English atmosphere as possible, or engage an Indian woman and chance the haphazard life an Ayah could offer? We chose the former and no one was allowed to touch her except Dukharan.

The fear of dysentery, cholera and numerous other diseases common in India was forever present in our thoughts. Malaria we could control fairly safely as the bungalow was regularly cleared and sprayed with DDT. She always slept under the net. When she wakened and fussed, I would sit in the soft glow of the night-light worrying. Among the din of howling jackals and beating drums, my ears strained for the hum of a mosquito. Every one I saw or heard carried the dread disease.

The servants watched me faithfully boil the container that held her bowls and spoons each day, never quite understanding why. Had I been able to show them bugs actually crawling over her utensils, and told them they must be boiled until the bugs disappeared, then and only then would they understand. Even Dukharan plunged his hand into the cooled pan to pull out a bowl he thought I needed. He must have thought me mad when I angrily marched out to re-boil the whole works again. Long past the sterilizing stage, I continued to do my boiling and countless toys ended up misshapen and ruined. Judy was well enclosed in a glass case and I found it difficult to get her out.

The dhobi could never be trusted with her linen. I had seen their ghats by the riverbanks. The scene had sickened me, as I visualized her clothes mingling with other people's dirty wash, being beaten on rocks and spread on the ground to dry. So, Mike sent to England for a small washing machine. It was the first in Mirzapur district, and it drew many admirers as it hummed on the veranda.

After we had covered Judy's crib with the net at night, Mike and I stood at either end straining our eyes, looking to see if we had trapped a mosquito inside. Satisfied that all was well, we went to bed ourselves where I would lie worrying and wondering over the speed of the fan.

"Ours was much too fast," I thought, "Surely hers wasn't much slower?"

And so I would slip out of bed and pad silently into her room.

"It was too fast, or was it?" turning the fan slower, I would stand anxiously by her side for a while.

"No, that was slow, maybe if I moved her cot away a bit and speeded up the fan again?"

After moving the bed, I'd untie the net and lay my head by hers to test it. There! That was better! But Judy, more often than not, woke up with a howl as a result of all this fussing. The whole procedure of tucking her in, changing the speed indicator and watching for mosquitoes had to be gone through again. Mike usually had had a good two hours sleep before I finally got to bed for the night.

Gradually, life took on a tranquil pattern. In the evening, the sun fell into the river, leaving a riotous sky of flaming red and we sat on the lawn watching the colours fade to muted shades of pink. This was when time stood still, the hour for our first drink while all living creatures around us were strangely quiet before the haunting sounds of an Indian night begin. The lights from the bungalow made soft patterns upon the grass. If turned your head a little sideways, you could see lazy activity taking place in the house.

Suleiman was flicking the rugs in the drawing room with his broom of twigs and bending to straighten the fringes by hand. Under the whirling punkah, Pir Mohammed set the small table for our light dinner and talked to Suleiman in his comforting musical voice. A tinkle of ice against glass and Dukharan stepped lightly down the steps with our drinks. He knew our mood and didn't speak as he set the tray by Mike's side and returned to the bungalow. A murmur of voices in the direction of the cookhouse told us that Ghulam and the chowkidars were also taking advantage of this magical hour and Gajada betrayed his presence by the glow of his "bidi" as he squatted near my bathroom door with his steaming cans of water. A child cried, but it wasn't ours; Judy was safely asleep beneath her net, watched over by her faithful Dukharan.

A fishing boat from as far away as Calcutta came slowly up the river, it's huge patched sail dyed pink by the setting sun. The voices of the men came over the water to us. A man went down the road singing. As it grew dark, we tilted our heads back and made silent wishes with each shooting star as it bursts across the sky. Then the fireflies came out to keep us company and to flit amongst the bougainvillea. We sprawled in our chairs lazily sipping and smoking. There was nowhere else we'd rather be than here, in our very own fairyland, surrounded by our very own people as the Indians quickly became as I grew to love them.

One afternoon while we waited for tea, we heard Mike send Suleiman for the body pusher. We knew now what the unpleasant odour was that had clung to the house all day and crept up our nostrils.

"Can we see, Mike?" I asked.

"I shouldn't, you won't want your tea if you do," he warned.

But hand-in-hand we walked slowly to the edge of the garden and nervously looked down. The bloated corpse of a man lay spread-eagled in the water below. Caught in a whirlpool, he lazily turned around and around while the vultures flew silently by, one by one, to roost in our trees.

"He was a poor man, as he's only singed. His family couldn't afford enough wood to have him properly burned," Mike softly said.

Down steps cut in the riverbank came a dignified looking old man with a long white beard. He carried a stout pole over his shoulder. The body pusher! Having seen enough, we hurriedly returned to the bungalow to refuse Dukharan's offer of tea.

We made new friends in Barbara and Pat Stokes from the rug-manufacturing village of Bhadohi, across the other side of the river from Mirzapur. Babs was a Londoner: smart, red-haired and fun. She possessed a delicious sense of humour, which brought new life to our club. Pat was Irish and ex-RAF. He was slight and fair and sported a huge orange moustache which he absentmindedly combed with a comb he kept tucked away in his breast pocket. Having no children, they got around more than we did. They were the sort of people that "things" happened to. While others could journey to and from Benares or Allahabad without trouble, Babs and Pat would invariably have punctures. They would eventually roll up to their compound in an ekka or a bullock cart, much to the despair of their rather staid employers. When they came to visit us by boat, Babs either lost her evening dress and shoes overboard or fell into the water herself. This set even-tempered Pat furiously to combing his moustache while he shouted orders for her clothes to be rescued, or hauled a dripping, giggling Babs from the muddy waters. When the weather was hot and dusty, they usually arrived late for the weekend with Babs' lovely red curls tied up in a pair of Pat's under shorts to keep the dust out.

Other visitors we always loved to welcome were Cecil and Olive Townsend from Benares. Both were as Yorkshire as the day they arrived in India twelve years before. Cecil knew about three words of Hindustani, "Yes," "No," and "Go," maintaining that if he lived there for fifty years, he would never master the bloody language. Olive, having to deal with the servants, spoke more fluently. At least it sounded good, until you discovered that it was spoken with a strong Yorkshire accent lavishly punctuated with "Luvs".

Two of the first things Olive learned when she arrived in Benares were that "Safaid" meant "white" and that "Memsahib" meant a European lady. One evening at the Benares Club, the bearer asked Olive if she would care for another drink.

"I'm drinking White Ladys," she told him, but he didn't understand. "A Safaid Memsahib, then," she said. Amongst hoots of laughter from the other members, the bearer departed.

"Well, he understood anyway," Olive retorted. But her face fell when he returned with a martini. Taking the drink from the tray, Olive looked up at the bearer and said "Eee, she's a bit tanned, isn't she, luv?"

The rains gradually eased off. We could feel the cold weather coming and smell it in the way the smoke from the village fires hung in the air. Sitting with our drinks before dinner one evening, Mike asked Diana and me if we would like to see Benares. Benares! The city I had read and heard so much about, the holiest city in all India, and one of the oldest cities in the world. Pilgrims came from every province in India to visit Benares, and it was the ambition of every Hindu to die there and be burned on her banks.

"I think you've been in India long enough now," Mike mused.

"Long enough? What do you mean?"

"Long enough to be able to take the sights and smells of the real Benares," he replied, "The bazaars, the burning ghats and the smell of hordes of sick and dying people. I want you to love it as I do. So you shouldn't see it too soon."

Early next morning we drove to Benares. We stopped for coffee at Cecil and Olive's bungalow on the outskirts of the city. After leaving Judy and Dukharan with them, we motored to the bazaar. I experienced an overpowering feeling of excitement as we passed pilgrims measuring their length along the road. They looked for all the world like inch worms, some having travelled in this weird fashion from all over India. Slowly, through narrow streets we drove. I leaned from my side of the car with a large old-fashioned curled horn, and squeezing the rubber bulb furiously. We honked and blatted our way through crowds of people, dogs, and cows.

"We'll leave the car here with Aziz and walk," Mike said as we drew to a stop. My heart was beating strangely as I opened the door. Without looking, I backed out of the car. Something made me hesitate, and looking down I saw a bundle of rags just below my outstretched foot. It moved, and looking more closely, I realized with a shock that it was human! Sticking out from the filthy rags was a head, a bare bottom and fleshless arms and legs. It was crawling with a million flies, up its nose and clustered about its poor face. The wretched soul was too weak to brush them away. I stood poised half in and half out of the car door. Seeing my horrified expression, people nearby burst into delighted laughter.

"He's happy, Memsahib," Aziz quietly told me. "He's dying in Benares."

Through narrow winding streets, we walked. My already shaky legs became weaker as we came face to face with a huge cow. We had barely enough space to squeeze by. Stepping gingerly over cow dung, we made our way down broad steps to the river to see the burning ghats. High piles of wood were stacked alongside the rows of shrouded stretchers that lay waiting their turn.

"The navel never burns, you know," Mike informed me.

"Never burns?"

"That's right, everything but the navel."

Before I had time to digest this piece of information, I spotted a man polishing a human skull to an eerie brightness. I clutched Mike's arm, "Whatever is that man doing?"

He's called an ogre," Mike told me. "They're the Indian black magic worshippers and do everything opposite to a devout Hindu, even they say, to eating human flesh!"

I shuddered. As he slowly rubbed the cloth back and forth over the skull, he stared at us with yellow eyes. People pressed about us. Beggars followed closely and the sickly sweet odour of burning flesh was overpowering. A suffocating feeling swept over me. I felt I must get away quickly to where the air was fresh, away from the staring crowd and frightful stench. One look at Diana's set face told me that she felt the same and Mike took us back to the car.

Perhaps it was too soon, for later I grew to love Benares as Mike did. We drove there many times to spend hours wandering through the bazaars and to watch the masses bathing and worshipping. At the day's end, we sat in the silk shops while they unrolled bolt after bolt of shimmering golden fabric for us to admire. More than one houseguest flatly refused a second trip to Benares. But one, very dear friend from Toronto, Jack Stevens, couldn't stay away. Whenever he was in India on business, he never missed nostalgic visits to India's holiest city. He had an excellent command of the language, for he had lived in India for many years previously. Armed with his camera, he would spend hours photographing and mingling with the multitude of people who gathered at the bathing ghats. Immaculate, with beautiful manners, and a delightful sense of humour, Jack was equally at home with the pilgrims, beggars and holy men at Benares as he was in the Savoy Hotel in London or the Waldorf Astoria in New York.

We three hired a boat one day. With a guide, we drifted down the river, and watched the people bathing or standing knee deep in the water staring unblinkingly at the fierce sun. We left the boat and climbed steps to the Nepalese Temple of Love. The guide took Mike to one side and said, "I'm afraid the Memsahib will have to stay behind while I take you and the other Sahib around the carvings. It is best that you take the Memsahib later, you understand?"

"Of course," Mike agreed. Leaving me sitting alone, they went off on their sightseeing tour. When they returned, Mike asked me if I would like to go with him and see the carvings. They were a little disappointing, he explained, being high up in the air and difficult to see.

I shook my head, "No, thank you," I replied through pursed lips.

"I have no interest whatsoever in pornographic etchings."

I minced off toward the boat while the guide nodded his head up and down in agreement. Tucked away in my purse were some photos of the complete works I had bought in their absence. While they had peered up at the carvings high above them, I had sat in comfort and examined each picture! No wonder the guide insisted I stay behind. One photo in particular would result in a heavy fine should anyone be caught with it in his possession in any other country but India. It was a couple's "first night." While busily engaged in the sex act, the mother-in-law stood by furiously fanning her daughter with a large fan.

Wanting some good milk for Judy, we decided to buy a cow. We drove to the mission one afternoon to inquire whether they had any for sale. As we turned up the long driveway toward Alan's bungalow, we spotted Winnie Wilson strolling down the drive under a pink parasol. Winnie was in charge of the mission's cows. Milking time would always find her keeping close watch, for Indians have the habit of half filling the buckets with water before they begin. The milk, besides being used in the Padre's and Missahib's houses, went to feed the babies in the Creche. But now funds were low and the mission was being forced to close this haven for unwanted children. One by one, the cows were being sold.

We stopped the car to chat for a while before Mike told Winnie what we had come for.

"A cow? Yes, of course. As a matter of fact, I have two for sale right now. Dear old Nhutkut and a younger one."

Winnie described Nhutkut in detail, but when Mike inquired about the younger one, she became noticeably embarrassed and began twirling her parasol around and around in the air as she desperately searched for words.

"She's—well, I mean to say,"—one more frantic twist of the parasol and she blurted out. "She's very difficult to get PG!"

"Yes, yes, I see," Mike murmured, sympathetically, while I cowered back in the seat and stifled my giggles.

"However," Winnie continued, visibly relieved to have done with the painful explanation.

"You must see them. No, I won't drive up with you. I have to call in at the hospital and will meet you in ten minutes by the cowshed."

We drove on and parked by Alan's bungalow in time to meet Alan and the other Missahibs coming out of the compound church. After chatting for a while I saw Winnie returning up the drive and saying good-bye. I left Mike talking, and went down to meet her. Drawing me beneath the shade of her parasol, Winnie took my arm and led me toward the cowshed.

"I shall be able to explain more fully to you, Mary," she said, and gazed anxiously at me, a worried expression in her blue eyes. Stopping just behind her bungalow and out of sight of the others, she proceeded to illustrate, all the while darting nervous glances over her shoulders in case Mike should suddenly appear.

"You see," Winnie went on, "When it's time I have her taken over the river to Bhadohi. Now that's fifteen miles away, as you know. When she gets there, well-she just sits down!"

"Sits down?"

"Yes, isn't it terrible? Of course, she's tired. I mean, fifteen miles!" and Winnie looked straight at me, to determine whether I fully understood. This seemed to call for some remark from me. I was tempted to admit that if I were forced to walk fifteen miles for the same reason, then I should jolly sit down also! Instead, I donned a very funereal expression and murmured,

"Yes, I see. That's awkward Winnie. Never mind, perhaps Nhutkut will do. Here's Mike now."

The three of us stood gazing intently at the rear ends of the two cows. The nearest I'd been to a cow that I could remember, was in the Livestock building at the Pacific National Exhibition held in Vancouver each year. Because it was the thing to do, my mother, sister and myself, nervously clutching programmes, made quick dashes up and down the runway between the stall lined with cows, fierce looking bulls and oversized horses. With great relief, we darted out the exit and onto less frightening exhibits. Winnie and Mike held a long discussion. The only remark I could think of was to say brightly, "Why, old Nhutkut here is the fattest cow I've seen in India yet!"

Mike looked at me scornfully. After a long pause, Winnie kindly said, "She's PG you see Mary."

We finally decided on Nhutkut and made arrangements to have her picked up when her stable was ready. Saying goodbye to Winnie we hurried back to the car, I felt I should burst if I didn't soon tell Mike why the other unfortunate cow seemed doomed to a life of celibacy.

In November, David took Natalie to Allahabad where they took a hotel room two miles from the hospital and settled down to wait. One evening a week later, we heard a car tear up the drive and screech to a stop with squealing brakes. A car door slammed and Dukharan in his usual jungly way hollered—"Logan Sahib atha hai!"

David galloped into the room, threw his long arms around me and kissed me on the cheek with a resounding smack. Then holding me at arms length, he announced dramatically

"It's over! We have a son!"

"How's Natalie?"

"Fine, just fine." David flung himself into a chair and sat hunched up, running his fingers through his curly hair.

"What's his name, David?" I asked.

"Robin, and he was born on your birthday, Mary."

"Whiskey soda pani lao," Mike shouted but Dukharan was already entering the room with the tray.

"You look like you could do with a drink, David," Mike said.

"Yes please, Mike. I've had a time I can tell you."

Mike nodded his head in sympathy while I sat staring at the two of them.

"What happened, David?" Mike asked as he handed him a large whiskey.

"Well, we were having tea in the hotel when Robin decided to arrive. While the woman who runs the hotel looked after Natalie, I jumped into a bicycle rickshaw to fetch Dr. Barar. We got half a mile down the road when the chain came off. I paced up and down while the man put it on and we started away once more. Further along, the damn thing came off again and would you believe it? Four times in that two miles, he had to stop to fix it, four times! You can imagine how I felt!"

"I can imagine how Natalie felt," I murmured, but they didn't seem to hear me and sat staring at their drinks, shaking their heads from side to side.

I hid a smile as a vivid picture came into my mind of David, the harassed father-to-be, being borne away in a rickshaw to fetch the doctor, the coolie peddling like mad and the chain flipping off every few blocks. Into my mind also came the picture of the streets of Allahabad teeming with rickshaws and ekkas.

"Why didn't you get into another rickshaw, David?" I asked.

Both David and Mike stared soberly at me for a moment until I almost felt mean at bringing up the question.

"Get another one?" David finally said, "Why, d'you know, Mary, I never thought of that!"

"I'm going in for chickens," Mike informed me one day, "These piddling little eggs get me down. Do you know we use between 20 and 30 eggs a day? What do you think of the idea?"

"Not much," I replied. "Chickens are stupid things from what I've heard of them—They don't know night from day and they always end up dying from some obscure poultry disease."

"You'll think differently when you have big English eggs for breakfast."

"The snakes will get them," I said.

"Not if it's properly organized. Anyway, you don't know anything about it. Don't forget you're a city girl and I was brought up on a farm."

Books and pamphlets on poultry began arriving through the mail. In our already over-crowded shelves, books on Mike's other current crazes: tap dancing, Yoga, canoeing, "How to Play the Uke," mountain climbing, flying and pig sticking were pushed aside and poultry took their place. Our walks around the garden were hurried now and always ended out by the motor house where the men were building the chicken run. Mike, book in hand, spouted at great length on the merits of raising your own poultry.

"Now, the run will be here," and Mike paced it off. "Do you think it will be large enough?"

"Plenty," I assured him, not having the slightest idea how much exercise a chicken should have. Nor did I care. I was bored stiff at the very sound of the word 'chicken.'

"There will be a hole made here," Mike pointed to a place in the wall of the motor house, "and on the wall inside there will be padlocked box where the hens will sit. I've already lined up a man from the village to look after them and he will keep the key."

"That'll be lovely for them," I answered absently. My mind was elsewhere. I was planning what to wear at the club dance on Saturday night.

"Now the hens will be put inside at night and a stone will block the hole, keeping them safe—You're not listening! Aren't you interested?"

"Oh yes, of course I am."

"I don't believe you are."

"Yes I am, honestly. Why don't you have a trap door instead of a stone, it would be safer don't you think? You know, snakes and things," I finished lamely.

"I know what I'm doing, the stone should be adequate."

Mike whipped out a piece of string dotted with knots, the Indian way of measuring, and began lining up the hole.

"Don't forget you don't really know anything about this sort of thing."

"Don't want to," I muttered. Then I brightened up. "I'll admit I didn't know Nhutkut was pregnant, but I know far more about hens than Sylvia does."

"How come?" Mike asked.

"Well—Henri was doing a sketch of a village scene and he couldn't seem to remember how to draw a chicken. So, he asked Sylvia to do one for him, which she did. But it didn't look right. It was ages before they realized that she had given the chicken four legs!"

"How absurd."

"Don't you think that's funny Mike?"

"Not really, any fool knows a hen only has two legs."

I gave up. When Mike was on to a new project, which happened every few weeks, he had a one-track mind. He ate, slept and lived that project until it was finished. I might as well face up to it. Until this particular phase had ended, I was a poultry widow and that was that. The eggs arrived and were placed in the box under some broody hens from the village.

Late one night, a dreadful squawking from the hen house awakened me. I put on the light and woke up Mike.

"Mike, there's something wrong with your chickens."

"It can wait until morning," he mumbled.

"Your chickens, Mike. Something's getting your chickens!"

Mike's eyes flew open. "My chickens?"

Grabbing a flashlight, he shot out of bed and up the path to the motor house. I lay listening until I heard the car roar out of the compound. So, I got up, put on a dressing gown, and peered out into the darkness. All was silent—what ever could have happened? Maybe a snake had bitten one of the chowkidars, and Mike had taken him to the doctor! I looked about the quiet room nervously. Then the car returned at a great speed and stopped at the hen house. In the light from the chowkidar's lamps, I could see long shadows leaping about and heard Mike yelling "Uska Mar Uska Maro" Hit it. Hit it.

I made a pot of tea and waited until Mike came dejectedly back to the bungalow. He sat awhile with his tea and then the story came out. When he rushed out to the chicken house, the stone was rolled away and three hens were loose in the run. Without the key he couldn't open the box to see what was wrong, so he shoved the hens back through the hole, blocked it up again, and drove off to the village to get the key. He had shut the chickens in with a wild cat! Four hens were dead and all the precious eggs were smashed. When he ordered the chowkidars to kill the cat, he had forgotten for the moment that they were Hindus and therefore wouldn't kill anything. So there they were, jumping around, smashing at the ground with their lathis but always feet away from the animal, while Mike grew more angry with each blow.

"Bloody chowkidars," Mike muttered as he drank his tea.

Poultry was never again mentioned in our house. Should anyone raise the subject, Mike quickly changed it. The books on 'Chickens' were shoved to one side and a volume, called "How to Install Septic Tanks" took their place.

16

Khamariah

BILL WALLIS, the managing director of our company lived at Khamriah with his wife Bimla and their two daughters Leila and Tara. Bill was from Yorkshire and Bimla a Bengali who had spent most of her years in England. Bill knew every one of the thousands of weavers on the company books and spoke Hindustani in the dialect peculiar to the Mirzapur district.

Khamariah is a spot unlike anywhere else in the whole of India. The big bungalow, as it is always called, dates back to Mutiny days and was built with part of the huge fortunes made from indigo. It was in this stately bungalow with its splendid pillars and broad verandahs that Brandford Sahib wrote the letter that started the carpet industry in the Mirzapur district, bringing to the people in the surrounding villages a life more secure than that to be found elsewhere in other provinces.

The upstairs was called the "Honeymoon Suite." To reach it you either used inside stairs from the veranda, or climbed wide concrete steps from the garden up the side of the bungalow and across the roof. The suite consisted of one spacious room, a smaller dressing room and two bathrooms. The floors were covered with a cream and green fitted carpet. The drapes and furniture covers were heavy off-white hand woven cloth. The doors on two sides of the main room opened onto a flat part of the roof that was enclosed by a low wall.

Downstairs had large airy rooms. Suspended from the ceiling of the nursery hung a huge pull punkah. The rope from the punkah ran out through a hole above the door and outside. Squatting on the veranda, a small boy patiently pulled the rope to and fro while the punkah swept back and forth across the room, creating a gentle cooling breeze. During the cold weather, fires burned in every grate throughout the bungalow. The garden was the loveliest of all. During the floods of 1948, waters of the Ganges covered the land from our house right up to the top steps of the Khamariah bungalow.

When they receded, it left the soil rich and fertile. One couldn't believe that a garden as beautiful existed outside of a fairy tale. Hollyhocks just didn't grow to the height of 15 feet or carry blooms as large. Sweet peas in every conceivable colour were massed along one side of the lawn. Each flower was easily three times larger than those in other compounds. Two high slender palms grew before the bungalow, planted by Bill and Mike twenty years before and from their green fronds hung the tiny perfectly woven nests of the Weaver birds.

Bimla always put us in the Honeymoon Suite whenever we stayed in Khamariah for the weekend. Her perfect servant Nazir awakened us each morning as he pulled the ropes of the mosquito net room that hung around our beds. Slowly the fine netting rose. When Nazir had secured the ropes, it hung from the ceiling in graceful folds high above our heads. Placing a tray of tea, iced juices and fruit by our beds, Nazir would set a match to the fire before seeing to our baths. Taking the tray outside to the roof, we'd sit on the low wall and watch the compound come to life below us. Factory workers, carrying long lathis, began coming to work. Far away, dotting the rough roads that ran through the green fields, weavers appeared bringing their carpets in on the backs of camels or in bullock carts. Smoke drifted up from the tall chimney of the dye house. Punwasi, Bimla's mali, gathered dew-laden flowers for the bungalow. Away in the distance lay the Vindya Hills, geologically one of the oldest ranges in the world. Unseen hands placed your favourite soap in the bathroom; filled bowls with your best-loved flowers. Beside your bed lay the latest novel. At every meal there appeared the food you especially fancied, some prepared by old Ali Jan in the cookhouse, the rest cooked by Bimla in her up-to-date kitchen off the dining room.

Bimla dressed in shorts or slacks as she went about the house by day, but always wore an elegant sari at dinner, one of the hundreds that hung in the massive wardrobe in her dressing room. She wore beautiful topaz jewelry designed by Bill and tucked a gardenia in her dark hair.

Conversation sparkled around Bimla's table. She was well read, widely travelled and witty. The servants silently padding in and out of the room serving deliciously prepared food, as we dined by candlelight. I listened entranced to the tales of the India under British rule. Names of fascinating places dropped casually from the lips of the guests: Cairo, Rome, Tehran and Kashmir.

After a stay in Bimla's well-run house, I always returned home fired by enthusiasm, determined to run our bungalow more efficiently. We even had the tea towels and dusters marked with the days of the week and I handed out fresh ones every morning. Here was a foolproof system of assuring that the dishes would be dried with clean cloths. But it wasn't long before Dukharan was drying the dishes with Tuesday's duster on a Monday and Pir Mohammed was dusting with Friday's tea towel on Wednesday.

17

Second Summer

NATALIE AND DAVID planned their leave in Edinburgh. Bimla and Bill packed for England, and Sylvia and I wrote to Mussoorie. We booked two suites in Rosehill, a house also owned by Miss Teddingwell that stood above and behind Hillcrest House. Judy at eight months continued to thrive despite the fact that I carried on being altogether too fussy over her.

Sylvia and I gave up trying to sleep in the overheated train around 2:00 AM. We dragged old Beat from her basket and made pots of coffee, enough to last us for the rest of the night. We sat hunched on the edge of the bunks. Old Beat sent forth gusts of evil smelling smoke and we drank mugs of equally evil-tasting coffee until we looked out to see the hills in the distance. Leaving the mess for Dukharan to clear up, we retired to the bathroom and tidied up before Mike and the children awoke.

Rosehall was the house Miss Teddingwell should have sent us to the year before, had she known in time that we were carpet manufacturers and not missionaries. Sylvia's suite looked out onto the snows. Mine, with its broad veranda facing the plains, overlooked the garden.

Although I fitted comfortably into the tub, it leaked. Thus, taking a bath required set timing. I'd call the Pani wallah, undress, slip on a dressing gown and take up my station by the door. When the outside door closed behind him, I'd rush in, lock it and take a flying leap into the tub before all the water ran out.

It was always exciting when a husband was arriving from the plains. Naturally, it's better if he's your own, but if not, it's still fun to look forward to someone else's. You lend things to one another, count off the days with them, and then send them away in a rickshaw all dressed up like a new bride. When they've returned to the boarding house, everyone embarrasses the poor man by peeking and staring at him. Although they always looked good to their wives, they usually looked tired and dirty from their journey, with the hot weather pallor upon their faces. All the other women looked at one another as if to say, "Is this what all the fuss was about?"

Now that the rains had broken, the house was cold and miserable. Sylvia and I hoarded all the orange peel we could find, dried it, and used it to coax the wet wood in our pokey little fireplace. Wrapped in sweaters and housecoats, our feet resting on hot water bottles, we sat huddled before the fire each evening warming ourselves with hot drinks made on old Beat. The thin cotton duri covering the floor billowed up in waves from the draft coming through the cracks. To cross the room whenever a strong wind blew outside, felt like ploughing through a desert of sand.

In August, Mike, Dukharan and Chipso arrived for a week's holiday before leaving for home. Chipso for one was glad when the week was over. She must have sensed the panther near-by that had already carried off eight dogs from the hotel up the road.

18

Mad Dog and Man Eater

We hadn't long been settled in our own bungalow again when Mike found it necessary to move the whole household over the river to Khamariah for the duration of the rains. We were all loaded into a big old riverboat and we headed for the village of Chilh on the opposite side. The river was swollen from the monsoon and was a dirty grey. Bodies of cows and dogs swirled by, disappeared down whirlpools, and popped up again. I held Judy and Chipso tightly to me and nervously eyed the frayed pieces of rope that tied the oars to the boat. The men struggled and grunted, their brown bodies glistening with sweat as they fought the strong current. Chilh drew slowly nearer. With a sigh of relief, I watched men wade out, grasp the boat and pull her into shallow waters.

We settled down in Bimla and Bill's lovely bungalow for weeks of perfect seclusion. We didn't have a radio, and the paper was often days late. As many of the roads were practically impassable, we had few visitors. Barbara and Pat braved the roads for the odd weekend. Outside of them, the only people we saw were the servants, weavers, and factory workers.

One afternoon, we were returning from our walk, we spotted a mad dog close by the bungalow. Ignoring Mike's advice to walk slowly and not attract the dog's attention, I tucked up my skirt, called Chipso and pushed Judy's pram before me. I tore up the driveway at top speed. As I galloped by an opening in the hedge, the dog lunged at me. It missed and collapsed in a heap. From far away, I could hear Mike yell for a pig-sticking spear. I lifted Judy from her pram and sped up the stairs. Past the astonished servants, I sailed on into the bathroom. With the vivid picture of the dog's crazy eyes and foaming mouth in my mind, I proceeded to scrub a frightened Judy all over with strong carbolic soap.

"Whatever are you doing that for?" I looked up to find Mike standing in the doorway staring down at me. I pushed the hair away from my face with trembling hands, suddenly embarrassed and feeling a little foolish. Then I remembered, a pig-sticking spear. How horrible—of course, all Bill's guns were locked away and Mike must have had the unpleasant job of finishing the poor animal's agony. Deciding to justify my existence and do something sensible for a change, I rushed off and poured him a double whiskey.

Babs and Pat roared up one Saturday afternoon to spend the weekend. After tea, Babs and I walked around the compound with Judy to watch the rugs being clipped and carved. The wool-drying women were hanging out huge hanks of beautifully coloured wool to dry in the sun. They gave Judy wide toothless grins as she presented them with flowers from a bouquet she had picked.

There was a massive Tamarind tree in the company compound. I always examined it closely, for the legend is that when it dies, there will no longer be any Europeans in Khamariah. Under the tree lay one of Judy's greatest friends, a huge tattered old camel. One of the weavers used it to carry his carpets. We went over to see him, but he lay quite still.

"Do you think he's dead, Barbara?"

While I held Judy's hand, Babs ventured closer to the camel and stared at it.

"I don't know, maybe he's just sleeping."

A procession of corpse removers, armed with stout ropes, entered the compound and headed for us, removing all doubt. So, we took Judy away to watch Mike passing carpets. Dozens of weavers squatted around the carpet floor. Mike, bathed in perspiration, was crawling over each carpet on all fours, digging his fingers into the pile estimating whether too much or too little yarn had been used. Then the carpet was flipped over for Mike to count the stitches. Chairs were produced, and we sat criticizing and admiring, as carpet after carpet was unfolded until we were dizzy from the beauty of them. Later, we sat in the office having a lemon drink when a clerk came to say that Gajada was waiting to speak to Mike.

"Send him in," Mike said.

Gajada, our old pani wallah, sidled in.

"Could the Sahib give him money for a doctor to see his daughter-in-law?" he wanted to know.

"Your daughter-in-law?" Mike asked.

"Yes, Sahib, she's very ill."

"Now listen to me Gajada, this firm pays the medical expenses for the staff and their immediate relations. What's the idea coming in here asking for money for your daughter-in-law? Your son, doesn't to my knowledge, work for our company. What's wrong with him anyway? He must be lazy—tell him to get to work and earn enough money, then he can look after his own wife."

Mike rose to his feet, leaned over the desk and glared at Gajada.

"But Sahib—."

Mike held up his hand. "Say no more, old man. Go now and tell your son what I have said."

"But Sahib—he's only 9 years old!"

Later, while we were putting Judy to bed, I asked Mike what had happened to the camel under the Tamarind tree.

"He just died. Old age, I guess. They came around taking up a collection to buy the man another one."

"How much did you give?"

"Not an anna."

"Why ever not?"

Well, take the long view of it. If I gave money from the Company we would have people from miles around bringing their half dead animals—cows, bullocks, and even elephants—just to die in our compound, don't you see?"

"No, I don't see," I retorted. "A camel must cost a fortune. I think it's very mean of you and really thought you more generous than that!"

"Generous? I bought a bottle of wine to pour down his throat when we were trying to revive him. At least it died happy." Mike added as an afterthought.

"I don't care, what's a measly bottle of wine?" I went into my "poor man" routine, glanced around to see how it was working and caught a rear view of my old man, hurrying through the rain to catch the cashier before he left the office.

When the rains ended, we returned to find that white ants had taken up residence in our bungalow. The man left in charge had been ill. Instead of doing something about it, simply sat around feeling sorry for himself while the ants spent the whole of the rains tunneling through the walls and floors of the entire bungalow.

The garden was as beautiful as ever. I spent hours examining the tiny green shoots that would very quickly turn our compound into a riot of colour. Wandering around the garden one day before tea, I idly kicked about a white object. I played football with it from the rose garden clear across the lawn to the riverbank before I discovered, with a shock, that it was the top of a skull! Good heavens, I thought, it may have been someone I had once known. What a dreadful way to treat an old friend. But I couldn't just leave it there. One couldn't have the top of somebody's cranium lying about one's garden, so I picked it up and went to put it in a little-used part of the garden on the riverbank. I squeezed past the bougainvillea hedge and into a sunken plot of grass under an old jackfruit tree, and stood looking at the peaceful view of the river. Here was the very spot to lay it to rest. Then my eyes fell on a lot of other "white objects." I had discovered a jackal's hideaway. Lying about in the long grass were the tops of over twenty-eight human skulls. The white ants in our bungalow were bad enough, but this was too much. Mike gave Mahdeo a severe dressing down for not attending more closely to his duties.

Everyone arrived back from their leaves: Natalie with a whole new wardrobe of lovely clothes, and Bimla and Bill with something very exciting in the form of a tall, good-looking Canadian boy. Ian Hampson suddenly decided to sell his old jalopy and, with the money, went to England. He read Bill's advertisement and was chosen out of hundreds of replies. Before he had much time to think about what he had done, he found himself out in India, 10,000 miles from home, learning to be a carpet manufacturer. Ian moved into the guest room on the riverside and fitted into our household as if he had always been there. We were sorry when the time came for him to move across the river to the small bungalow in Khamariah, just as Mike had done 20 years before.

The Raj Kumar Vizianagram of Benares invited us to a dinner party he was holding in honour of Sir Ivenlaw of the Indian Air Force and his wife, Lady Chapman. We climbed the steps of the palace to where the Raj Kumar and his wife waited. I caught my breath as I looked up and saw the way the light shone upon the Raj Kumari's jewels. She was dressed in a beautiful green chiffon sari. Her dark hair was drawn tightly back from her finely molded face and coiled in a shining chignon. Around her neck lay a magnificent necklace of huge square cut emeralds surrounded by blazing diamonds that matched the pendants hanging from her ears. The Raj Kumar relieved his sober black Indian formal dress by enormous diamond buttons in the jacket.

I began mentally composing a letter home. "Wait until I tell them this," I thought. When I looked down, I found myself treading on a carpet of tiger skins that lay on the entire length of the stairs. After a few polite words to our host and hostess, we were escorted by colourfully uniformed bearers to the ballroom, stopping on the way to look in a glass case that contained a stuffed family of tigers: Mother, Father, and two round curly coated cubs. The sight sickened me. I turned to Cecil and Olive who had visited the palace many times before, and said, "The Raj Kumar must have shot a lot of tigers. That long rug on the stairs and now this," as I gestured toward the case.

"He's a great Shikari," Cecil answered "With over seven hundred tigers to his credit."

"Over seven hundred? I can't believe that any one man has shot over seven hundred tigers!"

"Come and look at them," and Cecil led me into the huge ballroom.

High up around the entire room hung tiger heads, hundreds and hundreds of them. Two massive beasts stood at the far end of the room. On the center of the floor lay an enormous rug of perfectly matched skins. The floor around it was littered with skins, presenting a real obstacle course to the guests as they carefully picked their way over and around the raised heads. Two bearers did nothing else all evening but straighten the rumpled skins, while other padded about serving drinks from heavy silver trays. The room was filled with dark ornately carved furniture. Hanging from the ceiling was an ugly chandelier made up of blue glass butterflies.

After we had each, in turn, been presented to Sir Ivenlaw and his charming wife, the glass doors on to the veranda was opened to disclose the pipers. We were piped upstairs to dinner. There I found myself drinking champagne from a golden goblet, and staring at a scraggly little head of the only tiger in the dining room.

"That's a miserable specimen compared with the others downstairs," I confided to my dinner partner.

"It was a man eater," he replied. "The only man-eater amongst the lot, and it very nearly cost the Raj Kumar his life."

The dining room did seem to me an odd place to hang a man-eater and I suspected the Raj Kumar of having a macabre sense of humour. I felt pity for this head, but was filled with a greater sadness when I thought of the hundreds of beautiful beasts downstairs. I wondered what it was all for, what a dreadful waste of God's creatures.

19

Leave

I BEGAN TO EXPERIENCE the worry and excitement I had seen others go through. It was 1951, the year of our home leave. The two main things during the weeks preceding your departure were, I found, to keep your children from getting chicken pox, measles or some such illness, and yourself from becoming pregnant. One didn't go home for six months all pregnant, it just wasn't done. Imagine after writing excitedly about tigers and emeralds, drifting down the moonlight Ganges by boat and wandering sylph-like through your own orange groves—fancy turning up pregnant? Your ungainly figure encased in an unbecoming dirzi-made dress, lunging about on swollen legs and slopping around in flat brown leather sandals—it would never do. So, for weeks before you leave, your friends watch you closely, and whisper personal questions in the club john. If you were the least bit anxious, they promptly invited you to tea the next day, only instead of serving tea, you got gin.

Our day to leave arrived after a few close shaves and Judy in perfect health. Early in the morning, we set off by boat for the opposite side where a Khamariah car waited to drive us to Benares. High up on the bank at the foot of our garden, we could see Ian with Chipso watching anxiously beside him. Down the river, Natalie stood on her bank waving one of Robin's diapers. After taking thirty-five days to get out to India in the first place, five days to get home by air sounded like nothing at all, Mike and I both agreed. We should be home before we knew it. Five days isn't long, but it can be an eternity in the air or hanging about air terminals with a lively two-year-old child.

From Benares we took off for Calcutta accompanied by a flock of vultures, which wasn't, I felt, a very auspicious beginning. From Calcutta we flew to Singapore, a journey I won't forget in a hurry as Judy bit pieces out of a drinking glass. Next, we dodged a spectacular electrical storm before landing. Leaving Singapore, we flew on to Jakarta in the Dutch East Indies, where we sat hour after dreary hot hour before we took off for Darwin, Australia. In Darwin, we sank gratefully into beds, but had no sooner fallen asleep than we were rudely awakened, dragged from our beds, bundled into the plane. We were soon droning on toward Sidney.

By this time, I had decided that I definitely disliked flying. Not only was it uncomfortable with Judy sleeping stretched out across our laps, but also I was frightened. Although I nonchalantly buckled my seat belt at each take off or landing, and gazed disdainfully out of the window, or played with Judy, inside my stomach churned with fear.

I decided that I wasn't the only one and played little games with myself guessing which of my fellow passengers felt the same. Those that lay back relaxed in their chairs, looking out the window with half-closed eyes, were like me: watching the propellers to make sure they were still going around. Did they hate the International Date Line as fervently as I because it added an extra day? Every time the pilot strolled through the plane, did they expect him to make a dramatic announcement about failing engines and being calm and brave? I was willing to bet that a good many of them felt exactly the same, but they kept it well hidden. As I gazed at my calm reflection in the window, I figured I did, too. From Sidney we bumped our way through rough weather to the Fiji Islands for dinner. From there, started on our way to Canton Island to refuel.

This plane had berths and Mike, Judy and I shared a bottom bunk. Being limited in the amount of luggage, and meaning to re-charge my wardrobe in Vancouver and London, I had very little with me in the way of clothes. By this time, I was sharing Mike's pyjamas. He wore the bottoms and I the top that sported a long jagged tear down the back. With the lecture of "Ditching in the Pacific," still fresh in my mind, I fell asleep only to be awakened by a loud explosive sound as the plane dropped in an air pocket. Mike, Judy and I flew up and hit the top bunk. The plane shuddered, faltered, and then, as the props again began biting into the air, we lurched on. I sat shivering and holding Judy tightly to me with the vision of ditching in the sea vividly in my mind. And me, attired only in a torn pyjama top! Quickly I dressed in my last fresh sun dress I had been saving for Honolulu, then lay back and tried to sleep.

The plane flew on through calmer weather. "I shall look awful," I thought, landing in Honolulu in a creased dress. So, I struggled into the pyjama top again, and hung the dress neatly on a hanger. I drifted off to sleep, but was awakened by the curious actions of the plane as we hit bad weather again. My ears began to pop. "Good," I thought, "He's going up above this awful weather, we must be at least 20,000 feet by now." All of a sudden, the plane gave a violent bump and the engine cut out! I shot up in bed, grabbed Mike and hollered,

"My God—What's that?"

Mike gazed at me sleepily and said,

"Whatever's wrong with you? We've just landed in Canton Island." But the shock was enough to send me changing again and I spent the rest of the night in my dress.

Honolulu was teeming with ultra smart women and tanned, handsome men. We wandered along Waikiki beach, Mike ahead of me with Judy on his shoulders, while I lingered a few paces behind, frankly staring at the expensive beach outfits and stunning bathing suits. My Suzette's suit of ice-blue satin was passable, but only just, I decided, as I looked hungrily at the bikini-like suits these women wore. Mike had on his black wool trunks (nice wool, bought in London just before the war). With the sun hot on my neck, I fell to dreaming of the new clothes we would both buy when we got home. "Mike must have a pair of these loud trunks they're wearing now," I idly thought when something caught my eye and pulled me sharply from my daydreaming. The seat of his suit was full of moth holes!

"Mike," I whispered fiercely, "Your suit's full of moth holes and your bottom's showing through!"

"Really?" he answered. "That's odd. I haven't had them long. Never mind, I expect I'm the only person on this beach with nerve enough to do it," and he strolled on.

That night we boarded the plane for the last stage of our journey. The pilot circled the city and then headed out across the ocean on the longest air hop in the world. "There's nowhere to come down," I thought morosely as I watched the water below. My tummy had that knotted up feeling once more. We sat chatting with our fellow passengers and after a couple of drinks, the distance didn't seem quite so great. Then the plane lurched. We ended up in the aisle a tangle of legs, glasses and kids. “Here we go again, “Mike sang out cheerfully, “Let’s turn in, I’m sleepy.”

Sometimes, I felt, it was maddening being married to such a good-natured man. One who could sleep anywhere, at any time, under any circumstances. I came quite close to hating him at that moment, as I watched him drop off to sleep. Judy stayed wide-awake and raring to go. Still on Indian time, she was ready for five or six hours of good hard play at 9 o'clock at night. She tried to climb out of the bunk; I yanked her in. The plane pitched and tossed and Mike snored on. I got mad, lifted my fist and gave him a hard punch in the stomach. He opened one eye—“what did you do that for?” I began to cry, “You don’t care, I’m scared, I’ll never see my family again. Judy won’t settle down and San Francisco is still seven hours away!”

San Francisco has always looked good to me, but never better than that lovely morning when our wheels touched down on the tarmac. We re-fueled and then took off, flying over the most beautiful scenery of the whole trip. The lights flashed, “Fasten your seat belts,” and I looked down on Vancouver. We were home. Judy fell asleep as soon as we arrived. She slept a straight sixteen hours while my Mother and Dad, longing for her to awaken, kept creeping in to stand looking at her.

Vancouver had changed in only three years. It sprawled farther out and up. Old business establishments had disappeared and strange new names took their places. Suzettes was gone, and the building was now a broadcasting studio.

Three months of meeting old friends and taking trips to the beautiful islands on BC’s coast soon passed by. Two days after Judy’s second birthday, we took off for England. We toured England in a hired car, had a bang up do with Barbara and Pat in London, and then we were winging our way on back to India. Below us lay Delhi, her wide streets set out in great circles. We made a smooth landing and as I unbuckled my safety belt for the last time, I said to Mike,

“Thank God we’re safely back, as long as I live, I shall never set foot in another plane.” It’s just as well one can never look into the future and see what lies ahead.

20

goodbyes

CHIPSO REFUSED to let me out of her sight, and followed faithfully wherever I went. She had been mated with a German shepherd before we went on leave and had six puppies. Ian had given all but two away to good homes, keeping one for himself and one for us. Chipso proudly led me to a poor miserable pup covered from head to tail with eczema.

"We've tried everything," Ian told me. "They've all developed this disease which seems to come from the father. The city vet has tried ointments and a course of injections but nothing clears it up." Chipso was clear of it, so one evening Suleiman placed a big dish of meat and chapattis on the lawn. As the puppy was finishing his meal, Mike shot it cleanly through the head.

I was stroking Chipso's smooth coat one day not long after, when I found a lump on her back. My exploring fingers found another and yet another. I found to my horror that she was covered with them. I hurriedly sent for Mike and we drove down to the city vet.

"What a strange looking animal," he said, as we stood looking down at her.

"She's a Doberman pinscher and very precious to us," Mike told him. "Do you know what it is that she has?"

It was obvious that he didn't, for all he could say was that she was, indeed, a very strange looking dog. We drove home with heavy hearts. She continued to grow worse while Mike poured over his books on the care of dogs.

"The car's waiting outside, darling. You and Judy go over and stay with Sylvia for a while."

I knew what Mike was going to do and left with a sad heart. Sylvia met me at the door.

"May I stay with you for awhile, Sylvia?"

"Of course, Mary, come and have some tea. Is there anything wrong?"

"It's Chipso. Mike's going to chloroform her."

"Oh Mary, I am sorry. Couldn't he get someone else to do it?"

"No, he says he must do it himself." We sat until it began to grow dark.

"I had better go now," I told Sylvia. "It must be over and Mike will be upset." But when I returned home, Mike was still out by the motor house with Chipso and the servants were standing about on the veranda. Suleiman who looked after Chipso, stood alone. Mike walked quickly down the path.

"The chloroform the vet gave me isn't any good."

Taking his rifle down from the rack, he returned to the motor house. I was walking up and down the riverbank when I heard a single shot. I went quickly back to the bungalow and found Mike in his dressing room. He put his arms around me and we both cried.

"Suleiman must not bury her. Let the chowkidars do it and don't let them tell us where they put her." So, Chipso was buried in the garden that night.

"Send him to the hospital!" I heard Mike say.

"Who's that, Mike?"

"Husani the chowkidar, he's ill with pneumonia. I'm very worried about him. He's an old man, you know—I'm off now to see that my orders are carried out." He drove away hurriedly.

So, old Husani was ill. What price the Bloody Chowkidar now? Husani had the best of care, and when he was well enough to return to work, he was taken off night guard and put on the bird-scaring job where he could sit in the sun all day.

Our new chowkidar was a young Brahmin named Raj Kumar, intelligent, clean and a yogi of sorts. Whenever we had guests to stay, Raj Kumar would put on a show for us. While he knelt by himself saying his Pujah, or prayers, the servants dragged out a heavy bed of nails and placed it on the lawn. Raj Kumar finished his pujah amidst dead silence, and then, rising, in a dream like state, he walked slowly over to the bed and stretched out upon it. Boards were placed on top of him. Three men began leaping wildly up and down, higher and higher, landing on the boards with sickening thuds. Then a heavy bullock cart was produced, or failing that, a motorcar and driven slowly over him. When the boards were removed, Raj Kumar rose up and came over to show us the smoothness of his back. Not one nail had pierced his skin. Then, he passed around a four foot iron bar ¾" in diameter. After the men in our party had closely examined it, he placed the tip against a cloth pad covering his eye. He placed the other end of the bar on a thick board and pushed. Slowly the bar bent until it was almost double.

What was his secret? The bed of spikes I had secretly examined many times as it lay out by the motor house. No one had ever succeeded in bending any of the bars he used. "The Pujah, he always says beforehand," the servants assured me. I was beginning to believe they were right.

Natalie and David invited us to dinner, and leaving Judy in Dukharan's care, we drove down to the stone bungalow. Mike got out to open the gates at the end of the driveway. I sensed something was wrong the moment we entered the bungalow. While we sat with our drinks, Natalie suddenly blurted out—"We're leaving India!" I stared at her open mouthed, "Leaving India?"

"Yes," Natalie explained, "While we're young enough to start afresh in another country. We're worried about Robin's education, we could never be separated from him, and feel it's better to leave now than later when he's school age."

Being apart from your children was the biggest drawback to India. Although we had put Judy's name down for a school in England when we were there on leave, I refused to think about the day we would have to part with her. I pushed the very thought from my mind.

"Whatever shall I do without you?" I wailed selfishly.

"Where are you going?"

"To Canada."

"Not Vancouver!"

Natalie nodded her head.

"Well, that makes it a little more bearable, at least we shall see you while we're on leave."

I have always been cowardly about saying goodbye to those I love, and stayed home the morning they left. Natalie sent me a note. While I was reading it, I heard the train hoot and knew they were away. I was beginning to understand what Mike had meant when he told me that India was a country of goodbyes. I felt terribly alone.

Every year with frightening regularity came the plague scare. The old bubonic plague of London flared up at the end of the winter, and only died down when the hot weather arrived. Years before, during one of the worst epidemics, whole villages were left deserted as the people moved out to live in the fields until it was safe to return to their homes. That year, dead rats were found in the Khamariah bungalow itself. Bimla and Bill watched the tree rats in their garden race across the lawn, flip over and die before their eyes, they moved upstairs to live in the honeymoon suite. Whenever they ventured outside, they wore high boots. For to leave their feet exposed was to leave them exposed to fleas to bite them in the ankle.

"There's plague in Fatqhar village," Dukharan informed me. "Five people have died already."

This I knew was likely to be an exaggeration, but enough to set my heart racing. An overwhelming feeling of panic swept over me. Across the river, funeral processions wound their way along the sands to the burning ghats. The wailing of the women, the chanting of the men and the monotonous thumping of the drums came clearly across the water. Thin spirals of smoke curled up as they set light to the pyres. As we lay in bed at night we could see the glow of the fires. Judy, seldom out of my sight, was watched more closely now.

"There's plague in Bisundapur village," Ghulam told me. "Eight people are ill." Hour by hour, day by day, the rumors grew and spread. One morning Mike came home unexpectedly from the office and casually said, "The doctor's coming this afternoon to inoculate us. I don't think there's anything to it, but there seems to be the odd case of plague about." The servants and malis assembled on the verandah. Like children they shuffled their feet, giggled nervously and peeked around the door at the doctor as he unpacked his bag in the den. Judy, Mike and I were done first. Then the doctor worked on until everyone in the house and compound was inoculated. The servants went back to work and then one by one they appeared with khaki-coloured faces to ask if they may go home, as they felt ill. I sent them off, Mike went over the river to Khamariah and I was left alone with Judy. The serum never seemed to affect her, but to me, it was the worst inoculation of the lot. Dizzy, weak with nausea and with a raging headache, I stumbled around the bungalow after Judy as she trotted happily about at play. "If only she would stay in one spot for two minutes," I thought as I collapsed into a chair on the verandah. I lay back watching her through half-closed eyes. In the garden, I could hear an odd rustling sound. But the effort of getting up to investigate was too much, so I ignored it. There it was again! Judy and I were the only ones there. What could it be? Finally, I dragged myself out of the chair. Leaning wearily against a pillar, looked out into the garden. Vultures! Ten, twenty, thirty vultures I counted all roosting in our trees. Waiting. For what? The way I felt at that moment, they could easily be waiting for me. Ill as I was, the humour of it suddenly sent me into a fit of helpless giggling. I could almost hear them as they stared down at me with their cold evil eyes. "WE'VE CUM FOR YOU!"

21

rosamond baba

THE BUNGALOW was in a turmoil as we packed for the hills again, this time to stay at "St. Goar," a boarding house nearer the center of Mussoorie and run by Gran Johnston, a wonderful old lady well into her seventies.

Out came old Beat to be cleaned and filled. Out came my maternity clothes to be aired and pressed. I had already booked in at St. Mary's hospital up the hill behind St. Goar. I wasn't prepared for it to be perched right on top of what turned out to be a very high hill. It had the annoying habit of appearing long before you reached it, only to disappear as you plodded along and appear again in a tantalizing way, long before you finally turned in at the gates. But it was worth the hard climb as I discovered when the matron, Sister Vincent, took me on a tour of the building. A veranda encircled the whole building. One side displayed a breath-taking view of the snows, while the other overlooked Mussoorie and the plains. To reach St. Goar from the Mall, you climbed down a steep hill, passing the YWCA Hostel and a Catholic convent on the way. An oblong block of concrete sat outside the gates of the YWCA. The words "Bear ye one another's burdens" were engraved on it in Hindi. The coolies rested by it on their backbreaking climb up the hill. I passed an exhausted coolie there one day with his load tipped back on the block. The strap around his forehead loosened for the moment to reveal a deep mark in the skin, and a refrigerator in a heavy wooden parking case upon his back.

Gran gave me one of the cottages set a little apart from the main house and we settled down to await the Nanny who was coming up to look after Judy when I went into the hospital. Sifting through twenty-eight replies to his ad, Mike chose a Miss Gimble from Saharanpur. She was to have a bedroom and a bathroom in our small-overcrowded cottage. I wasn't too happy at the thought of sharing with a stranger. Judy and I walked down the road to meet her early one morning.

"What will she be like?" I wondered. Then I spotted a skinny woman mincing up the path followed by three coolies. Two carried her luggage, while the third trailed along behind carrying her umbrella and knitting bag.

"Miss Gimble?"

"Yes, Mrs. Norbury?"

"That's right, how do you do?"

She extended a limp hand and looked beyond me and over my shoulder. I took an instant and violent dislike to her.

"This is Judy. Say hello to Miss Gimble, Judy."

"No."

So, Judy felt it too. I could hardly blame her for her unusual rudeness.

"One thing I must tell you Mrs. Norbury. I smoke." Miss Gimble gazed past me at a tree.

"That's alright," I told her. "So do I, when I'm not expecting a baby. But I do hope you won't smoke while attending to Judy."

"Oh no!" she said. "I wouldn't dream of it, I do hate to see smoking while looking after children."

But on Judy's morning walks, Miss Gimble sidled out like a crab, eyes averted, and a box of matches peeking out from under the hanky clutched in her hand. During her hours off, she retired to her room and chain-smoked while I sat and listened to the continuous scraping of matches. I felt ill from the odour of stale cigarette smoke. Lying awake one night listening to her having a bad coughing attack, I had the awful thought that she may have TB, so the next day I sent her up to St. Mary's for a check up.

The examination showed her free of any disease, but I once more took over the care of Judy while Miss Gimble knitted. The pile of cigarette butts grew outside her bathroom door.

"I can't stand her another moment longer," I confided to Wyn Knight in the opposite suite.

"I don't blame you, Mary—neither could I."

"Whatever shall I do?"

"Wait for Mike to come up," Wyn advised. "It's only another few days and he'll know what to do.

Mike and Dukharan arrived and Judy and I were waiting down by the road and his first question was—"How is the Nanny?"

"Awful, Mike!" I blurted out, "You must send her away."

I could tell by his face that he thought it was my "condition" that was making me so difficult, but he hadn't been in the cottage five minutes before he agreed she must go, immediately.

"She gives me the creeps, why can't she look you in the eye?" he asked.

Even Dukharan gazed at her suspiciously and took Judy out for a walk, casting reproachful looks at Mike and me as he left, holding Judy's hand protectively. So, after two weeks holiday in the cool of the hills, a free medical and a month's pay, Miss Gimble returned to Saharanpur rested and refreshed.

Sister Alma, my doctor, was an American nun. We sat talking in her office one day when she suddenly surprised me by asking when I would like to have the baby.

"What do you mean?" I asked.

"Well, you're tired of climbing these hills, I know. You name the day and I shall simply make a small adjustment."

I thought back to my long wait for Judy. "Would Thursday suit you?" I asked.

So Thursday it was. Early in the morning, little Rosamond arrived and Judy had her longed-for sister. Back at St. Goar, I found that Mike had hired Sister Drury, a fully trained nursing sister. Between Sister Drury and Dukharan, a friendly feud arose.

"Rosamond baba has a lovely head of hair," she would croon.

"Judy baba had more," Dukharan would snap back.

Rosamond baba very seldom cries," Sister Drury would say.

"Judy baba *never* cried," and taking Judy, he would march off. In time, he grew to love Rosamond, but Judy remained his first love.

During the rains, clothing was difficult to dry and shoes and leather goods grew mouldy overnight. A tin tub was up-ended over a charcoal fire in the bathroom. All Rosamond's essential washing was draped upon the warm tub, while Judy's clothes were pegged to a line stretched across the bathroom. I went to great trouble one day to arrange the diapers and sheets so that they dried quickly only to return a short while later to find that Dukharan had pegged all Rosamond's things to the line and put Judy's on top of the tub.

We left for home and took Sister Drury with us for a two-week stay before she returned to her home in Lucknow. I sure played the Memsahib on that trip. Mike took Judy over, Sister Drury had Rosamond in a separate compartment and I lounged on the top bunk eating biscuits and reading detective stories—I was taking advantage of a nurse while I had one.

22

Memsahibs

MIKE'S SISTER ROSAMOND came out to spend the cold weather with us. A great party of us spent Christmas in the jungle. Bimla ordered a huge tree from Naini Tal and sent out a kerosene fridge and a cow. Fresh fruit and vegetables were driven out from our gardens every other day. Those with children lived in the stone inspection bungalow, while the others lived in tents. At night, we sat around a roaring campfire with blankets covering our knees. The servants squatted nearby in groups, gossiping in quiet voices and getting up to build up the fire or re-fill our glasses.

At home, waiting for Judy, was a playhouse the carpenters had made with a Cape Cod door, windows hung with green and white checked curtains and a carpeted floor. I had made a rag doll "Agnes." She wore Judy's cast off clothing and sported freckles and red carpet wool plaits. From a Muslim friend of ours, Hakimuddin Khan, came a dear little white pony named Binky.

Our stay in the jungle ended and we reluctantly left for home. The only member of our party who was glad to leave was Gaffor, Bill's driver. He rolled up his bedding and found he'd been sleeping with a nine-foot baby python all night! As Mike's sister Rosamond and I wrote home to tell of our camp holiday, the python grew longer with each letter as snakes often do until it reaches at least eighteen feet.

Dukharan's old Dad died, so Dukharan appeared one morning with his head shaven, except for a top knot, left there for the purpose of pulling him into heaven should the occasion arise. He had a nail in his Lotah. After seeing to the burning of his father's body like a dutiful son,

Judy on her pony Binky with Dukharan and a mali (rear).

he must wander about unclean for at least two weeks, he explained, and do no work until the period of mourning was over.

"Laloo will do your work," I told him.

So, Dukharan went home. Against all the rules and regulations of the Hindu religion, he spent the two weeks finishing off his new house. When the work was completed, I asked Dukharan if I could take the annual photo of his family and look over his new home. So, we set off through the village one day before tea.

In a little hut at the beginning of Bisundapur lived a pretty friend of mine named Bhudni. She had just borne a son that morning. I left Dukharan outside and, with a basket of fruit and vegetables, I entered Bhudni's house. She squatted by a small fire and hastily got to her feet.

"Don't get up Bhudni, I've come to see your son," and I squatted by her side. Bhudni reached over to a string bed and pushed aside a dirty smelly pile of sacking. Beneath sleeping peacefully, was a perfect little boy. The black Khol was already smeared around his eyes and a string encircled one fat little wrist. I took Bhudni's hand and she gazed at me proudly.

"Well done Bhudni," I told her.

I didn't say what a beautiful baby he was as the gods may visit some dreadful disease upon him, so I just said he was a little rascal or words to that effect, but Bhudni could tell by my face how I felt about him.

Dukharan and I continued on through the village. The usual custom was for Dukharan to walk a few paces behind while I was supposed to call back over my shoulder if I had anything to say to him. Ignoring this stupid habit, Dukharan and I walked side by side while he told me all the village gossip.

"See that man by the well in the Brahmin village, Memsahib? He murdered his own mother."

One family looked out of place—they all had blue eyes, fairish skins and tawny coloured hair.

"They've always been like that," Dukharan informed me, "Away back to their grandparents."

This must have come about, I thought, from the days long ago when Mirzapur was a military station. A British tommy in the bright red uniform of those times, must have found one of Bisundapur's maidens irresistible. The village school was in the middle of afternoon lessons. Little boys sat cross-legged on the veranda with their slates before them chanting their lessons while the schoolmaster squatted by the side of the road answering nature's call.

Women came to their doorways to salaam and hold up their babies for me to see. The number of children who followed us grew as we passed through the village until dozens of them, all salaaming loudly, were trailing along behind us when we reached Dukharan's new house.

"What a wonderful house, Dukharan." And, indeed, it was. It boasted two stories and a smart red tiled roof. The whole family had gathered. Dukharan's wife took me in to see her new daughter-in-law, leaving the men of the house outside, as they weren't permitted to look upon her face for two weeks. The house was built around a courtyard. Huddled in a corner was the slight figure of a girl. I jumped when a green parrot screeched a welcome from a cage hung in the yard, we all gathered around the new bride. A hand whipped out and tore the sari from her face. She stood, eyes downcast, while the other women all gazed at me expectantly. Whatever was I supposed to say? She was so pitifully young. How homesick she must be, I thought. She was away from her family for the first time and among strangers. There was a hushed silence and the women continued to wait for my reaction. So, to be on the safe side, I put my head on one side, examined her from her head to her hennaed feet and murmured in English, "Hmmm, she'll do, yes, she'll do just fine," which seemed quite in order as they covered her up again, and called Dukharan in to show me the house.

We climbed a bamboo ladder to the upper story and peeked into a windowless room. Glancing over his shoulder to make sure he wasn't overhead, Dukharan whispered,

"This is my Memsahib's room." I peered into the dim, airless room. It was devoid of furniture and smelling damp and musty.

"How very nice Dukharan, your Memsahib must be pleased to have a room all to herself."

This was part of our own special language. Whenever I enquired after Dukharan's wife, I always called her his "Memsahib," but only when we were alone. The other servants would have teased him unmercifully. A Memsahib is a European lady, and they always referred to their wives as "my woman."

Now for the annual photograph. The size of Dukharan's family multiplied yearly from his sons bringing home new wives and from the arrival of his grandchildren. Half the village had gathered outside the house. While I tried to remember Mike's instructions on lighting, Dukharan lined his family up in front of the doorway. He stood back and inspected them.

"Ready, Dukharan?"

"Han, Memsahib."

"Just a moment, Dukharan. Dasrath is missing."

Dasrath, their youngest and my favourite, was found hiding in a tree. He was hauled down and pushed roughly into position and Dukharan stood back and inspected the group once more. Then he rushed forward and grabbed two children by the arm. He peered into their faces—they weren't his! Discarding several grownups and children this way, the photograph was finally taken. Mike printed it and I proudly presented it to Dukharan and his "Memsahib." They held it upside down and both exclaimed delightedly, "Bahut saf hai!" (very clean).

23

the season of catastrophes

ALL TOO SOON, it was time for Rosamond to return to England and for us to go to the hills. There was no sense of foreboding in my heart as we sped along toward Dehra Dun, this time comfortable in an air-conditioned carriage. We were leaving old Beat home for the first time. Judy made great friends with the attendant, called him "Uncle Wiggly," and carried on long conversations with him in Hindustani. Rosamond played and slept the journey away safely tucked in a canvas cot the carpenter and Dirzi had made for her. I relaxed with my detective magazines.

Gran gave us a large suite downstairs in the main house. Mike left a servant named Laloo with me to help with the children. Laloo had turned out to be an excellent helper and was devoted to little Rosamond. He was a bearer to be proud of, tall, fair skinned and handsome. He wore little gold rings in his ears, and kept his uniforms immaculate. He was only 19 and had left Bisundapur for the first time, leaving behind his tearful old parents and a beautiful little doe-eyed wife.

The house and cottage soon filled with people. Liz, a Dutch girl from Indonesia, and her two little girls Erica and Yolanda took the cottage we had the year before. Eve Hartley with her two children, Tina and Robbie, occupied the suite next to mine. Next to them, lived Marjorie Reid with her four daughters. Upstairs, Beryl Goodman and her daughter Brenda took the suite off the dining room. Although other families came for short stays, we originals stayed on. It was a season of catastrophes: everything went wrong from the very beginning. Sickness among the children was the main problem. No sooner did one child come down with a cold, than it went right through the whole house. When the last child had recovered, the first would develop a tummy upset. And so, it started all over again.

Our pocket money was swallowed up in pills, doctor's bills and building-up tonics. Our cupboards were overflowing with medicine. We seemed to spend our time with Dr. Spock's book of *Baby and Child Care*, under our arms, going from room to room offering advice or sitting with an anxious mother while she waited for the doctor to visit. Gran was very patient and somehow arranged special diets without any fuss. We often went to her for advice, knowing she had raised five children of her own without Dr. Spock. We couldn't imagine how she had ever done it.

Eve, Beryl and I shared a small table in the dining room. One evening, while we devoured huge juicy mangoes, Beryl told us of her work in a hospital in Delhi.

"I work for the most wonderful man," she said. "He's an Englishman out here on the Colombo Plan, teaching Indian doctors orthopedic surgery."

"What's he like?"

"His name's Dr. Roaf. He's tall, ginger-haired and quiet, but a genius in the operating theatre. Once he took a crippled beggar who had been dragging about on his bottom for years. After several operations, the man is walking upright with the aid of crutches."

"How wonderful!" Eve and I exclaimed.

"Yes, it was, but the man complains that he now has no way of earning a living."

"He must be a clever surgeon," I said, little knowing what effect he would have on our lives.

The children behaved like little monsters, so much so that we were forced to put them in the kindergarten at the convent for a few hours daily just to get a little peace. We caught them once, down in Marjorie Reid's suite, with toothbrushes and powder, scrubbing out the thunder boxes.

Exhausted, we slung the lively kids into bed, poured ourselves a whiskey, and tried to relax while the children leapt up and down on the beds. Higher and higher, they jumped, louder and louder they hollered, while the springs creaked and the beds thumped against the walls. Would this year's stay in Mussoorie never end?

"Mary, do come and look at Brenda. I'm sure she has a fever." Beryl's worried face appeared at my door. Eve and I hurried upstairs to find a feverish Brenda tossing and turning on her little bed. One of us phoned Dr. Garg, a charming Indian doctor who often attended the children. We sat with Beryl as she waited for him to arrive. Dr. Garg examined Brenda, gave her a penicillin injection and left, promising to return in the morning. Brenda was ill for three days: sore throat, fever and headache. On the fourth day, she was better and up and about again. Next, it was Erica with the same symptoms but she, too, was soon better and ready for the journey home to the plains. Eve and I sat having tea in my sitting room.

"Thank goodness, Mike arrives on Monday. Only three days more. I'd rather suffer the heat than this any day."

"It's been a horrible three months," Eve agreed, morosely staring out at the endless rain, "and there will probably be a grand finale," she prophesied.

Sunday afternoon I sat sewing in the garden taken advantage of a watery sun while Judy played near by.

"Daddy's coming up tomorrow, darling. Then we'll be going home to see Dukharan and everyone. You'll be able to ride Binky again and have a lovely fourth birthday party in your very own bungalow."

"Mummie, I feel cold," and she turned a flushed face up to me.

"Oh no, not again!" I moaned inwardly, and put her to bed.

Watching out for Mike the next morning, I saw him hurrying along the path with a worried expression on his face.

"What's wrong?" he asked. "Why weren't you down to meet me?

"Judy's not well," I told him. "But I'm not worried, it's just something going through the house again."

But that night her temperature rose alarmingly and Mike ran up to the YWCA to phone the doctor. Dr. Garg was perplexed. He examined her, out came the penicillin and after the injection, he left, promising to call in again the next day. We spent a sleepless night while Judy grew hotter by the hour. Her breathing became laboured and she was delirious. The next morning, she was no better. While Mike walked up to the shops for books and toys, I sat and waited for the doctor

"Mummie."

"What is it, darling?"

"I can't move my leg!"

I flew over to the bed.

"Which one? Tell me, sweetheart. Show Mummie."

"This one," and she pointed to her left leg.

'Try love, try and raise it," and with a look of fierce concentration, she slowly raised it a few inches off the bed. It flopped back down again.

"It hurts," she whimpered.

I saw Dr. Garg pass the window and I rushed to the door.

"Judy can't move her leg, doctor!"

He sat on the bed by her side,

"Show me Judy. Try and lift it," but it was no use, she couldn't move it.

I gripped the bedstead and Dr. Garg and I stared at one another.

"Doctor," I whispered. "It can't be—," No, it couldn't be. At home, they had epidemics of it, but one seldom heard of it out here. Not polio, my mind cried out, after protecting her so carefully from malaria, plague and typhoid, must she have polio?

"No, no," Dr. Garg answered angrily, "I have never had a case of polio here. But with your permission, I shall get another doctor's opinion." and he hurried out.

Dr. Downie at the Landour Community hospital where Judy was born was phoned. "If it is polio, she must come into isolation. I can't get away to see her. You must put her into a dandy and bring her over immediately."

Mike returned, arms laden with books and toys and I met him at the door.

"Judy can't move her left leg, she has polio, Mike. I just know it!"

"Nonsense, I refuse to believe it," and he hurried into her room. I told him what Dr. Downie had said and he soon had Judy comfortably settled into Gran's own dandy. The coolies gently lifted it up. Mike holding an umbrella over her, they set off on the four and a half mile journey to Landour. I stood holding Rosamond closely to me and watched them out of sight. I fed Rosamond and put her to bed, waiting for the time to come when I could phone the hospital from the YWCA. One by one, the mothers came in to sit with me. Dr. Spock lay open at the "Symptoms of poliomyelitis," but no matter how I tried to twist Judy's symptoms around, they always returned to that dreaded word. I mended Judy's teddy for something to do, and then it was time to phone.

They let me speak to Mike.

"It isn't, is it darling?" I asked.

"Yes," he answered. "They've just taken a spinal and she was so brave through it. I told her the story of the three bears and she didn't make a sound." Mike's voice broke. He tried to say more, but couldn't. So, he hung up, leaving me staring at the silent, black receiver. I got up and slowly walked out; close by the front door I saw a room with a large cross upon the wall and I went in and knelt before it. Someone knelt by my side. It was Doris Chubb who managed the hostel. In a quiet voice, she prayed aloud, for I couldn't speak.

When I returned to St. Goar, all the girls and servants were waiting in the garden. They knew by my face. Eve stepped forward, put her arms around me, and held me close.

"Give me Rosamond, Mary. You go on up to the hospital."

Word had spread. A rickshaw manned by sober-faced coolies came down the hill as I climbed to meet it. The men refused to let me out to walk the steep parts, but with quiet voices bade me stay in. With each turn of the wheels, I sent up a prayer for Judy as we creaked slowly on. The bazaar I loved so well sickened me now. The roads were littered with mango peel, cow dung and pools of red spittle. How could I have ever loved it? I thought, imagining Judy, deathly ill, having to pass this way. Even the flies seemed to have increased by the millions. By the Tibetan shops, the coolies handed me into a dandy, and I was soon swinging up the path to the hospital. I looked down at the inscription I had read many times while waiting for Judy to be born.

"Landour Community Hospital, for the service of Jesus Christ, the Chief Cornerstone."

"Let her live, please Jesus," I prayed.

I was directed upstairs to isolation. On the second floor, a nurse came forward and I told her who I was.

"Sit here, Mrs. Norbury, you will not be allowed beyond these curtains. You've been told what your daughter has."

"Yes, I spoke to my husband on the phone."

"You won't be able to see Judy because of the danger of infection to your other daughter."

"May I see my husband?"

"No, he is going into isolation to nurse her. Here is a list of things he wants sent up. You may go outside and call up to the window and speak to him, I'll tell him you're here."

I gave the nurse Judy's teddy and made my way downstairs and outside. Mike was leaning out of the window.

"Hello darling, have they told you I'm staying?"

"Yes, how is she?" I asked anxiously.

"Now you must promise me you won't worry. I'll take good care of her—Judy, Mummie's outside." I heard her weak little voice. Then Mike said, "Go home now and have a rest. If you can leave Rosamond, try and come up in the morning."

When I arrived back at St. Goar, I found that Beryl had already been in touch with her husband John in Delhi, who in turn had contacted Dr. Roaf. The doctor suggested that all the fathers take their families back to Delhi by car and go into quarantine in their own homes, so that they should be near him in the event of further cases developing. We sat miserably in my sitting room. It was now all too obvious what Brenda and Erica suffered from. Each Mother worried to herself. Who, they wondered, would be next?

"We hate leaving you, Mary. It's rather like deserting," Beryl said.

"I should do just what you're doing were I in your position," I assured her. "Anyway, I shall have Gran."

That night Eve refused to let me sleep alone. She gave me a pill. Ignoring the bed Judy had so recently occupied, she slept alongside me in Mike's bed. Eve, who was terrified of creepy crawlies, imagined panther lurking outside her room at night and worried about countless imaginary things. It was Eve who rose to the occasion and I shall be forever in her debt. She contacted a nurse who was living at the YWCA and suggested she come to look after Rosamond, leaving me free to visit the hospital. But the fear of polio was too great and the nurse refused. Eve angrily told her off and marched back to St. Goar in a furious temper. The next morning, on shaking legs, I went up to the YWCA and phoned the hospital. I waited while they went outside and called up to Mike. Judy was still running a temperature.

"No change," they told me. Eve once more took Rosamond and I went up to the hospital.

As we jogged through the Landour bazaar, I heard the sharp RAT TA TAT TAT of the town crier's drum and heard him calling out—"SUNAIYE, SUNAIYE BHAIEN. KHABADAR! KHADADAR! BIMAR KE WAJA LARKIYAN DIASCOPE NAHIAN JANA CHHATA."

As the rickshaw drew nearer, I slowly translated his message.

"Listen, Listen, Brothers. Warning! Warning! On account sickness, children should not go to the movies."

The people crowded around him. Children clutching fly-covered mangoes and sticky Indian sweets stared solemnly at him and went on eating. They heard him warn—"Keep flies from your food, wash hands before eating. Listen, brother, Listen, RAT TA TAT TAT, there a sickness about, children should not go to the movies, Warning. Warning!" RAT TA TAT TAT. His voice and drum faded away as we journeyed on.

How frustrating it was to stand outside and call up to Mike. Our conversation was overheard by almost everyone in the building. How calm and full of faith Mike was.

"When Judy's better, you will have to fly the girls home to Vancouver where she will have the best of care."

"Can't you take us?" I asked.

"No, I shall have to work out my contract of eight months before I can leave."

"How is she, Mike?"

"Don't worry, she will be fine."

Thursday morning, Jack Hartley, John Goodman and Joe Reid arrived from Delhi to take their families home. We sat in Gran's sitting room, having tea before they left.

"I will see Dr. Roaf as soon as I get back to Delhi, Mary," Beryl said. "I'm sure you can count on his coming up to see Judy."

"All the way up here?" I asked.

"Yes, he's that sort of a man."

"Beryl, before you go, will you do something for me?"

"Anything, Mary."

"Please phone the hospital and see how Judy is. I'm frightened."

"Of course, I will. Right away," and she hurried out.

She returned a short while later and walked slowly into the room. Over the sound of the rain thundering down upon the roof, I heard her say, "Mary, love, the paralysis has gone into her right leg!"

I stood waving goodbye as they followed their heavily laden coolies down the path. Except for the incessant drumming of the rain, the house was strangely quiet.

"Give me Rosamond, Mary," Gran called out from her room, "and go on up to Mike and Judy." Friday, Sylvia, who was living farther up the Mall, came to look after Rosamond. I was grateful. That evening, I phoned again. A cold chill settled on my heart as the nurse said,

"Hold on Mrs. Norbury, the doctor would like a word with you." While I waited, wild thoughts ran through my head.

What did he want to speak to me for? What would he say? Was it all over? What would I do?"

Dr. Downie's voice came over the wire, "Mrs. Norbury." From far away, my voice came choking out, "Yes, doctor."

"Now Mrs. Norbury, before you come up to the hospital tomorrow to Judy, I wanted a word with you."

"Thank God," I breathed. Weak with relief, I clasped the phone with trembling hands.

"I wanted to explain to you as I have your husband," the doctor continued. "The paralysis isn't always lasting."

"I understand, doctor."

"I'm afraid, Mrs. Norbury, that the paralysis has entered her arms and hands!"

Into her arms and hands? Slowly it was creeping over her body. Where next? Into her chest? Not that. Please God, for there were no iron lungs!

Back at St. Goar, I found a wire waiting for me.

"Doctor Roaf and nurse arriving Mussoorie Saturday morning. Chin up, love Beryl and John."

Saturday morning, rickshaws were sent down to meet the doctor and his nurse. I waited at St. Goar to join them and accompany them to the hospital. I stood before the window watching the rain. A wild waterfall cascaded down from the Mall and roared past St. Goar in torrents. Laden coolies struggled up the path through the water. Their stout sticks slipped on the wet stones and their grunts were clearly audible to me where I stood above.

Finally, word came that the doctor had taken the higher road and was already nearing the hospital. My regular coolies were pulling the doctor's rickshaw. All other rickshaw coolies had disappeared from sight to shelter from the rain, so I hurried off alone. By the time I was slipping and sliding down the Kulri, the rain had soaked clean through my coat to my underwear. Oblivious to it all, I rushed on, almost running the miles to Landour. They allowed me to sit in the waiting room. Not until I heard a nurse address the other occupant as "Mrs. Roaf," did I lift my eyes to look at her.

"Are you Doctor Roaf's wife?"

"Yes."

"I'm Mrs. Norbury, it's my little girl your husband has so kindly come to see."

We chatted awhile and then a tall sandy haired man, accompanied by Dr. Downie, descended the stairs.

"Here's my husband now," Mrs. Roaf said. I went forward to meet him.

"Is there somewhere we could go and talk privately?" he asked.

"In my office," Dr. Downie replied. "Do you mind if I sit in?"

"Of course, Doctor, do by all means."

We sat silently a moment while Dr. Roaf examined his beautiful surgeon's hands. Finally, he raised his head, his eyes probing mine, seeming to determine just how much he could safely tell me. I must have made a discouraging picture as I sat huddled in the chair, nervously twisting my kerchief, while rivulets of water ran from it to join the pool gathering at my feet.

"In the first case, Mrs. Norbury, it is, as you know, polio. And a very severe case."

"She won't die, doctor?" I had never dared voice the word before.

Dr. Roaf hesitated, examined his hands again, and then gently said, "I can't say, only that the next three days will tell."

Three days! Another three days of waiting and worrying, but then five had already passed.

"If she lives, doctor, will she ever walk again?"

"She may walk with assistance, but never run."

Never run! Judy who seldom ever walked, but always ran. Pictures of her trotting about on her sturdy legs ran through my mind. Only the week before, I had caught her outside Gran's whirling about dancing to a gypsy band. Faster and faster, she danced while the gypsies played and laughed, loving the sight of her flashing feet.

"All I can say," Dr. Roaf went on, "is that she is having the best of care. We have tremendous admiration for your husband. If Judy comes through this, she will owe her life to her father's devotion. I shall make open splints for her legs to lie in, and then Sister Goff will take over and your husband can come out. Now come and meet Judy's nurse. After lunch, you may see Judy."

Lillian Goff from Delhi was a tall, pretty woman around my own age, with children of her own.

"I've seen Judy," she said to me, giving my arm a squeeze. "Don't worry, love. I shall take good care of her."

They took me upstairs beyond the forbidden curtains, helped me into a white gown, and led me into Judy's room. She lay pale and thin, both arms lying lifelessly on the sheet that covered the frame over her legs.

"Hello, darling. Mummie's going to take you and Rosamond home to Nana and Grandad?"

"Oh?"

She was too ill to care. I longed to cuddle her but she was in pain, so I just took her little hand.

Waiting by the rickshaw for Mike to join me after he had been "disinfected," I saw an apparition coming down the path. I peered through the mist and heavy rain. Surely, they wouldn't allow a patient out in this weather, I thought. But it looked like a patient. Someone should be told. I started forward when I discovered that the "patient" was my old man. Mike strode down the path in a pair of thin, cotton hospital pyjamas.

Only one button remained on the shrunken jacket and the sleeves hung below the elbow. The pants flapped about the calves of his legs, leaving a wide expanse of ankle. His feet bare of socks, looked huge in his brown brogues. The skinny striped pants gaped alarmingly in front. I shoved him in the rickshaw and pulled down the shades.

"Where ever are your clothes?"

"Hanging wringing wet out on the hospital veranda. They boiled them!"

"Boiled them? Your lovely grey Daks you bought in London?"

"Yes, and my plaid shirt and my beautiful hand-knitted socks. They boiled them all in a kerosene tin. The shirt and socks are ruined and my trousers have pink splotches all over them. But to heck with clothes, darling. How good it is to be with you again." Mike held me tightly to him.

"All this has been awfully hard on you, I know. The worry and trekking back and forth."

Never a word was said about the time he had had, the anxious waiting and sleepless nights while he watched Judy grow worse hour by hour. As we neared the center of town, I breathed a sigh of relief.

"I'll sneak you into the house somehow and then you can get dressed."

"OK," he agreed. "But hold on, I have to send a wire to Lillian Goff's husband so he'll know she's arrived safely."

"Not now!"

"Yes now. I promised."

I blushed as I watched him out of the back window of the rickshaw, climbing the hill to the Post Office. No one seemed to notice. Not one person even turned to stare and I know it wouldn't have bothered Mike one bit if they had.

Sunday morning, Mike walked up to the hospital promising to return for lunch so that I could go in the afternoon. A group of women from the YWCA passed by St. Goar and called out—"We're going to pray for Judy."

"Thank you."

A tall young minister knocked on my door and in a Canadian accent said, "I have just heard of your trouble and came to help."

Together we knelt in my little sitting room and prayed.

"There will be a great volume of prayer going up for Judy from the Hillside today," he told me. "All churches in Mussoorie and Landour will be holding special prayers and the ministers will be asking their congregations to pray in their homes."

Dr. Downie spread the word to the hundreds of missionaries living in Landour, asking them to hold special prayer meetings. Mother Superior at the Convent held Mass and sent a blessed medal for us to hang by Judy's cot. Hindus, Sikhs and Mohammedans prayed also. One old Muslim gentleman told me: "There are many paths leading to God Memsahib, you and I may travel along different roads, but we reach the same Almighty—I too am praying."

"No change." Mike told me when he returned for lunch. Not waiting to eat, I set off for the hospital. Climbing the steep part past the Tibetan shops, I sat to rest on a low wall and looked up toward the hospital nestled amongst the trees. I could see the window of Judy's room.

"Free yourself from worry and strain." the young minister had told me. "Let God's healing power reach you unchecked by doubting thoughts."

All of a sudden, I relaxed. The sun burst through the dark clouds to warm me. Instead of the desperate frightened pleas I had uttered before, I prayed calmly with all my heart, sending my prayers to join all the others that I knew were being said for Judy at that moment by hundreds of other people on the hillside. On light feet, I made my way to the hospital. After putting on my gown, I entered Judy's room to find Lillian, face beaming, and waving a thermometer at me.

"Judy's temperature is down, has been for the last two hours. She feels life in her arms and hands."

Mike and I took turns each day to visit Judy. Some days Mike journeyed twice. As he refused to take a rickshaw or dandy, he was walking nine, and sometimes eighteen, miles a day. But we had come so close to losing her, that every minute spent in her bare little room was immeasurably precious. Lillian refused to wear a cap and mask in case it frightened Judy. At night, she pulled the two beds together so that she could cuddle Judy when she wakened and called for me. She made dozens of beautiful little stuffed animals and tied them to the cot alongside the models she cleverly fashioned in plastercine. Mike or I would relieve her so she could visit the bazaars or go to a movie. But she wasn't happy leaving Judy for long, and soon returned carrying a gift for her. As we passed below the window, we could hear her singing to Judy. I began to take an interest in the bazaar again, poking about in the Tibetan shops for something to amuse Judy: a little ring of silver bells, bracelets, necklaces and boxes studded with turquoise and amber.

"Look Lillian—Judy's trying to pick her nose." Entranced, we watched her do the very thing I had always forbidden.

"Come on Judy, keep trying." One thin little arm made its shaky way toward her turned nose. She reached it while Lillian, and I hugged one another with joy! Letters and cables poured in from our homes across the seas and from friends from India. Mike began making preparations for our trip.

"Sister Vincent at St. Mary's Hospital has offered us a young Indian nurse to look after Rosamond. We shall have to leave the girls, the two nurses and Laloo in the hotel in Delhi while you and I go back home to pack. You fly from Delhi," Mike continued. "Lillian has agreed to go as far as London with you, then another nurse will be there to accompany you to Vancouver."

"How are we going?" I asked.

"BOAC Comet to London."

"Those new jet things?"

"That's right, lucky you."

"Lucky me? I swore I'd never fly again!"

Mike went on, "I've planned for you to stay in London for at least five days, in case there are any delays. See that you enjoy yourself and take in some shows."

Fifty days had passed since Judy entered the hospital. At last Dr. Downie gave permission for her to leave. Ian had arranged a special bed in the back of the station wagon, and Gaffer drove up from Khamariah. Armed with a special permit, he went on past the gates, and through the streets of Mussoorie, to park by the Tibetan shops below the hospital. Rather than send for Dukharan to see to our heavy luggage as usual, Mike sent for an office clerk. We both agreed it would be too upsetting for Judy and Dukharan to say good-bye. But, one morning he appeared at my door.

"Dukharan!"

"Salaam Memsahib, Judy baba kahan hai?"

"In the hospital where she was born."

He turned to go.

"Wait Dukharan, aren't you going to eat and rest first? It's over four miles away."

"No Memsahib," and he hurried off, his face full of sadness. They took Dukharan upstairs to a room close to Judy's and pushed her cot near the window. Lillian told me later that there was no question about his not being allowed to see her. There was a certain dignity in his bearing, something about the expression on his face and in his soft brown eyes. They granted his request without question.

Early the next morning, Mike left for the hospital. Laloo, Rosamond and I waited on the Mall for him to pick us up. Although it was very early in the morning when Mike drove slowly back through the streets of Mussoorie, shopkeepers were ready and waiting. Mr. Singh of "Singh's Variety Store" was sitting on a chair by the side of the road holding a doll in a beautifully decorated basket. He leaned in the back of the car and placed the basket by Judy's side, "Come back to Mussoorie soon, my little friend."

The man from the fruit stall presented her with a basket of her favourite fruit. One by one, our faithful rickshaw and dandy coolies leaned in the car to give their farewell salaams to Judy, then Gran's servants and finally Dukharan. Everyone, even the coolies, somehow sensitive to Dukharan's feeling, turned away and busied themselves with the luggage. And then, Dukharan, tears blinding his eyes, hurried off down the hillside.

Farther up the Mall, Sister Vincent waited with more toys for Judy, and to hand over Margaret, a shy slim Indian nurse with a long black plait hanging down her back. Judy took the long drive to Delhi very well, despite the fact that to move her legs or body even slightly out of line, caused her severe pain. Four air foam pillows supported her stretcher bed and cushioned each bump as Mike drove slowly and cautiously on.

That evening, we reached Delhi and trouped into the luxurious Ambassador Hotel. While Mike checked in and saw to the luggage, I secretly watched Laloo's reaction, for he had never been in a big city before and certainly never in a building like the Ambassador. There he was gliding gracefully about the lobby, giving instructions on the way to carry Judy's bed, and acting as if he owned the place. He looked a little puzzled when we stepped into the elevator. I wondered if he would react in the same manner as a servant of Brandford Sahib's when he first rode in an elevator in Bombay. He, so the story goes, left the lift several stories up, looked out of the window and promptly fell on his face and hugged the floor. Laloo, however, stepped lightly out, glanced through the window and continued on down to our rooms, never betraying for an instant the fact that he had come almost straight from a little mud hut in Bisundapur.

Mike and I journeyed by train to Mirzapur, back to an empty bungalow with the rugs still rolled up from the hot weather. Boxes and trunks lay ready to pack. Each morning I awoke, stretched and began to plan my day, only to realize, with a shock, that it wasn't the same. It would never be the same again. I packed the cases for our air journey. Into the trunks went the things for Mike to send on by sea. Then it was finished and time to return to Delhi. The servants lined up on the veranda.

"Goodbye Ghulam."

"Goodbye Memsahib, come back soon."

"Pir Mohammed."

"Goodbye Memsahib," in his soft, lovely voice.

"Gajada." I shook hands with each one. Mahadeo pressed a damp bouquet into my hand.

Dukharan stood by the car door and I took his hand.

"Goodbye my friend."

"Goodbye Memsahib."

I looked at him helplessly and then got quickly into the car. Tires spun on the gravel as we raced out of the compound. I never looked back.

24

the comet

IN DELHI, we found all was well. They had even taken Judy to Eve's flat for tea. Dr. Roaf visited us, accompanied by two nurses who made fresh splints for Judy's legs.

The night before we were to leave, Mike and I sat in our room having a nightcap. Judy had sung herself to sleep and lay on her stretcher bed with a smile on her little face.

"You're not worrying about anything?" Mike asked.

"Not one thing," I answered.

"Not even flying?"

"No. I feel strange, Mike. Don't think I haven't read about these new jets mysteriously blowing up in the air, or whatever they seem to be doing. But I believe my capacity for worry has been completely drained. It's a glorious feeling." I got out of my chair and curled up on the floor by Mike's feet.

"I've always wished I could be like you, never worrying about things until they happened, facing up to it and doing something about it. Like you did for Judy."

"You can't change your nature," Mike said.

"No, but something's changed me. From the moment of Judy's miraculous recovery that Sunday, I feel sort of protected, as if nothing can touch us now. We don't know what lies ahead for her, but we do know that her brain is clear, her arms and hands grow stronger every day, and we didn't lose her. What more could we ask?"

"The years here, and the friends we've made, I wouldn't have missed for the world. But the days for world trips and being waited on are over. The time has come to get down to the serious business of living."

"And you'll have to learn how to cook!" Mike finished for me.

The Comet was waiting sleek and beautiful in the sun. We stood talking to Beryl, John, Eve and Jack. Then the pilot joined us.

"Welcome, Mrs. Norbury, nice to have you with us. You may take Judy aboard now. We'll see you have a good trip."

"Thank you, Captain."

Lillian said goodbye to her family, and went ahead with Judy. Mike led me outside. The Stewardess took Rosamond from Laloo,

"Will you come aboard now please?"

Mike held me closely to him.

"Bye for now, darling. See you next May."

I entered the plane. The stewardess was strapping Judy's stretcher in place.

"Will you put cotton wool in the children's ears?" she asked. "The Comet makes a deafening noise when she takes off and it may frighten them."

I took Rosamond on my knee and buckled my seat strap. The plane strained powerfully and taxied slowly away. I caught a glimpse of Mike standing alone on the tarmac. Then with a tremendous roar, and a wild high-pitched scream, we were away. The Comet streaked off toward Karachi.

BOOK II

Judy's Story

1

to india

THE NINETEEN-HOUR-LONG journey from Vancouver to Delhi, preceded by months of intense anticipation and planning, had left me dazed and bewildered. As we finally circled the airport, all I could see through the plane window were a few yellow lights.

Ross and Belinda and I had been the first people to board the plane in Vancouver for the flight to Seoul. I transferred to a small-wheeled chair that fit into the aisle of the plane to get to my seat. Singapore Airlines was very posh. Each seat had its own TV screen on the back of the seat in front, along with a wide choice of movies, music and games. The flight attendants were beautiful and charming. They brought steaming hot cloths for our faces and hands before presenting us with each sumptuous meal. The flight was long. Twelve hours to Korea, an hour-long stopover in Seoul to refuel, and then 5½ hours to Singapore. We were surprised by the steamy tropical night as we left the airport there for the fancy hotel that was part of the price of the ticket. Most of the next day, we looked about the city. Singapore seemed modern, expensive, with none of the charm my mother discovered on her way out to India to marry my dad. For her, I said hello to the Raffles Hotel, imagining her dancing and flirting under the moon and stars. In the afternoon, we took the bus back to the airport for the last leg of our journey to Delhi.

I was numb on this last flight until we circled Indira Gandhi International Airport. Those lights below—that was India. I wept as I saw the lights coming closer. It was actually India down there. Would a rush of familiarity greet me when I first smelled the Indian air? Would I instantly recognize the language being spoken around me?

2

Vancouver Childhood

FOR ALMOST A YEAR after returning to Canada with my mother and sister, I had to stay in hospital. The somber skies of a Vancouver fall and winter were in sharp contrast to the almost constant sunshine and blue skies of India. I missed the warm dark faces of our house and garden staff, especially my very best friend, dear Dukharan, who had showed me so much love and caring. On one of her visits, my mother transcribed a letter for me to my father still in India.

Children's Hospital,
February 17, 1954

Dear Daddy,
I love you Daddy, you are a very nice Daddy. Are you coming in May? Is Dukharan coming? My mummy comes every visiting day. I love Dukharan. Is Raj Kumar coming out here to Canada? Is Pir Mohammed coming out too?

Mummy's hair is different, it's been cut—Daddy, do you like Mummy's hair? It has curls on the top.

Your loving Judy
XXX

The hospital was often a lonely and terrifying place. Visitors were allowed only three times a week, for an hour or two and children were not allowed to visit at all, which meant I never saw my sister. I was tied to the bed by a restrainer, a sturdy vest fastened up at the back with three sets of ties. On each side a long leash was tied down under the edge of the bed. I struggled in vain to unknot these ties so I could turn over. I hated being restrained. The regular physiotherapy was extremely painful, and I would throw up my breakfast on physio days from fear of what torture the session would bring me. Some nurses were kind; others were gruff, brusque and sometimes cruel. I underwent several surgeries in an attempt to align my body and legs, and I can still bring to mind the sickening smell of ether. Twice the doctors did what was called "stripping the hips," an operation that involved making a six-inch incision along each of my hips to cut the tendons, and incisions were also made below each of my knees, apparently to cut the bone and turn it so my feet pointed in the right direction. My hospital records no longer exist; so the exact procedures performed remain a mystery. The goal of them all was to fit my legs into straight metal braces.

Some respite came with the happy arrival of a case of measles. As the children's hospital was not set up to handle infectious diseases, I stayed at my grandparents' home with my mother for the duration of my illness. Nana and Grandad moved into a house my mother had rented house to be with Rosamond. That time for me was pure bliss. Nana's cups and bowls were opalescent pale-green glass and her polished enamel oil stove, with its red-needle thermometer behind a small glass window, shone against the black and white tiles of her kitchen floor. A bold-faced clock sat on the shelf above the stove, and clean striped dish-cloths hung from the drying rack. Sunshine streamed through the windows. Everything was light and bright, and life was good again.

Then came the crashing reality of having to return to the hospital. I screamed. I cried. I wept for hours in absolute misery at the injustice of it. After a day of anguish came bleak resignation. The only positive aspects of life there, besides my mother's visits and the presents she would bring each time, were the striped hard candy we got after our daily spoonful of cod-liver oil and the fact that each day we were allowed to choose a different starched dress, with puffed sleeves and a sash, from a rolling rack brought around by an auxiliary volunteer.

A device my family would later call the rack, was built for me towards the end of my stay in hospital. Constructed of canvas stretched over a metal pipe frame, its purpose was to prevent my spine from developing further scoliosis. Every night I lay on my side, sandwiched between two plastic walls. Under my side and ribs was a foam-padded support covered in grey naugahyde. The front removable piece of plastic was attached to metal rods that fitted into the main frame, holding me firmly in place. The leg on the underside was on same level as my body and the other was raised onto a canvas platform about eight inches over the lower leg and the whole contraption stood on seven-inch legs with red rubber tips. I was expected to sleep in this strange device, suspended there with no pillow. I was forbidden to raise my lower arm up under my head, though I always did it. As soon as I started sleeping in this thing, I began to wet the bed. I always had the same dream. Three plump cartoon mice would appear in a line, each in a vest of a different colour with rick-rack trim. I would look at these mice and count one… two…three…pee. It was exactly the same every night.

I was supposed to continue sleeping on the rack even when I was sent home from the hospital, and my mother bought a pair of toy handcuffs to restrain my arm. Every morning she would wash my sheets and air out the canvas. On weekends, I was allowed to sleep in my bed without the rack. It didn't take too many weeks for my parents to relent, and the horrible thing was cast into the basement.

A whole generation of my contemporaries endured similar bungling experimental treatments for polio. Polio is a viral infection that presents as an inflammation of the motor nerve system. It is a disease thought to go back at least 5,000 years. Before excessive hygiene became practically a religion, babies developed a natural immunity through exposure to the virus, found in fecal bacteria, and sometimes through contracting a mild case of the disease. Polio epidemics followed improvements to sanitation. The US experienced its first major epidemic in 1916, and further epidemics flourished in the years between 1944 and 1955 in North America, Europe and Australia. Babies were kept so clean that they developed no antibodies. This left them vulnerable to severe polio infections. All of my mother's washing, all her boiling, all her scrubbing of me with carbolic soap, to protect me from the germs of India may have unwittingly made me more susceptible to the thing she feared most.

It was the early fall of 1954 and I was five years old. My father had come back to Canada that spring, and my parents had bought a wood-frame house on Vancouver's east-side, on a street lined with maples. It was a thrill to roll in my new wheelchair through the crisp autumn leaves. They made a satisfying crunchy sound, as my mother pushed me through them. I loved the smells of autumn, too, decomposing leaves, rich rotting humus, the earthy smell of the wild mushrooms my dad loved to find and investigate, but would never eat. Big-bodied brown spiders hung suspended in their webs from shrubs sparkling with dew or the previous night's rain. Shimmering steam rose from rooftops and fences warmed by the morning sun.

During that first year home with my family I made a few return visits to the hospital. I fractured my leg after falling off a kitchen chair, and there were several short stays in the hospital's high humidity room to assist with the bronchitis I got every time I came down with a cold. The nurses in the steam-filled room wore shower-caps, gumboots and gowns over their starched white uniforms.

My family lived close to the neighbourhood where my mother had been born and where my grandparents still lived. My grandfather, who was a carpenter, built two illegal suites on the top floor of our house to help my parents pay the mortgage. A series of tenants moved in and out through the years. A self-contained room and bathroom in the basement first housed a middle-aged couple and then Gar, my paternal grandmother from England.

My mother, with her keen sense of beauty, colour and design, artistically arranged our living-room, with its fine Indian carpet, smaller rugs and patches of bare floor. Many pieces of furniture were antiques from my father's family estate in England—an ox-blood Victorian leather reclining chair; an ornate marquetry table with curved legs and an intricate inlaid floral design; a grand writing desk with large drawers below and many small drawers above, some with secret drawers behind them. This desk, with its musty Dickensian smell, had survived a sea journey from England to India, where it endured many a monsoon season, before being shipped to us in Canada.

My father's carpet experience in India qualified him for no job in Canada. After a miserable stint selling carpets door-to-door, he found a job at a used furniture and linoleum outlet, an offshoot of Woodward's department store. While working at this dead boring job, he studied hard for his industrial first-aid ticket. After working away from home to get the required six months' experience, he secured a job as a first aid attendant for the longshoremen loading and unloading freighters at the Vancouver piers. The union job was secure and fairly well paid, and it allowed my father to visit with sailors from all over the world. He would trade stories with them and bring tales of their lives home to us. My dad loved people from all walks of life. He was an avid reader and his keen and curious mind absorbed the intriguing details of everything he heard.

The struggles of my parents to make a new life in Canada in no way marred the idyllic childhood my sister and I shared. That I could no longer walk made no difference to my enjoyment of life. I had a small wheelchair but was more often on the ground or the floor, where I had devised a way to scoot myself about. The big old Gravenstein apple tree in our back yard produced the sweetest, most delicious fruit and the largest apples I had ever seen. There were Sunday country drives and picnics, holidays by the sea, a backyard swing set and a plastic pool I could almost float in. Summers seemed endless. The only hardship Rosamond and I faced was having to be in bed by 7:00 o'clock. On long summer evenings, we could hear the neighbourhood children playing kick-the-can hours after we'd been put to bed.

For my sixth birthday, I received a red leather-covered transistor radio that played rock and roll. The music excited me, and I happily sang along. My parents played everything from Broadway musicals to operatic arias on the record player and songs were always heard around the house and in the car. My mother had a beautiful voice. As she washed the dishes, she was a torch singer performing popular tunes and standards from the 30's and 40's: "Your green eyes with the soft light, your eyes that promise sweet nights..." and "When they begin the beguine it brings back the sound of music so tender..." Hymns soared effortlessly as she wielded the iron, pressing the aired laundry: "...and He walks with me and He talks with me and He tells me I am His own...." My dad enthusiastically sang English music hall numbers, Gilbert and Sullivan and naughty army songs with grunts and abbreviations in place of the rude bits. Rosamond and I puzzled over what might be missing.

"Old Mother HB, queen of all the fairies.
She's as clever as the Lord knows what!

She threw up a coconut, caught it in her *mm mm*,
Turned a double somersault and cracked it in her *hmm*!"

My grandad had a fine strong voice and entertained at parties with songs such as "The Whiffenpoof Song" and "Far Away Places".

In the fifties, children with disabilities did not go to regular neighbourhood schools. At six, I started school with other outpatients in the basement of the hospital. We were taken there each day in a bus driven by volunteer firemen. The school was divided into two classrooms; Miss Climie taught the high school group and Miss Robertson the elementary. We ate the hospital lunch, and on Fridays there was melted ice cream. After lunch, Murphy beds would be folded down out of the wall so that the younger group could take a nap.

I was very proud to be going to school. I eagerly learned to read and write, though I was always being told that my printing was not neat enough. Once I cried from the criticism, but generally I loved Miss Robertson. She wore her wiry grey hair in a long braid wound in a crown around her head. Sometimes she would put my hair into French braids. I'd squirm as I endured the painful tugging and pulling and Miss Robertson would tell me, "You have to suffer to be beautiful!"

From grade four on, I went to a regular elementary school closer to my home. As it was not policy in the public school system to enroll disabled students, Tommy, a former classmate, and I were groundbreakers in this regard.

3

my mother

BEFORE HER MARRIAGE, my mother had been one of Vancouver's top models, appearing regularly in hotel fashion shows and on the fashion pages of newspapers. A favourite photo of her was probably taken for her modeling portfolio. It showed my mother with her blonde hair pulled up smoothly and arranged in a pile of curls on top of her head, a rope of pearls wrapped five times around her neck. She was looking into the distance, thoughtful and composed, with only the slightest hint of a smile on her full lips. The photograph was reproduced in a June 1948 issue of the *Vancouver Province* and the article accompanying it read in part, "*One of Vancouver's most decorative models, Miss Mary Hargreaves, whose beauteous face and figure have frequently graced The Vancouver Daily Province's fashion columns, will leave here July 24 for India, where her marriage to Mr. Michael Norbury will take place.*"

I loved my mother intensely. "Mummy, do you know how much I love you? I love you to the end of counting, the end of counting times!" My greatest fear in life was that my mother would die. That fear may have come from the separation from her while I was in hospital, or perhaps I had taken on her fear of the possibility of my death.

My mother was five foot nine, tall compared to most other women. She wore her brown hair swept up into a French roll secured by three or four hairpins, no hair out of place. On occasion she would become a bleached blonde, or have a blonde streak with the same severe hairstyle. Her deep-set eyes, which sparked a dark blue, could pierce me with an eagle's stare. Before bed, it was always startling to see her, long hair down around her shoulders, her washed face shiny with scented Pond's cold crème, her lips pale, without her favourite lipstick, "Love That Red."

Mary with pearl necklace.
(photo by RH Marlow)

Her clothes were of good quality, in solid colours like navy, royal blue, and her favourite, lilac. She wore tailored blouses with skirts or trousers, accented by a string of pearls, a gold chain or a brooch, either the emerald and diamond piece that was my father's first gift to her, or a mounted gold nugget, a gift from my grandmother, Gar. Summer was a time for capris and sundresses. She had large hands, strong, capable and artistic. Her long fingers were sometimes adorned with more than just her wedding ring; her favourite was a large light-green cabochon emerald surrounded by diamonds that she loved to show off. My father gave this ring to her on her birthday while they were in India. It was a ring only a woman of my mother's elegance and bearing could wear well.

Back in Canada after living in India, my mother had to learn how to cook and clean and manage a household. She was a good basic cook. There were always plenty of vegetables, never over-cooked, salad, some sort of potato and meat, and fish every Friday. A couple of well-used cookbooks sat in the kitchen cupboard and I expect she occasionally called her mother for advice. She was not an enthusiastic, but rather, a dutiful cook. She excelled at desserts. She made rice pudding and bread and butter pudding and lemon snow and lemon pudding with cake on the top and creamy custard below and wonderful pies with flaky crusts.

My mother spent a great deal of time going up and down stairs to do laundry. One part of our basement housed laundry tubs and a wringer washing machine, plus a wooden clotheshorse and lines to dry laundry in wet weather. I loved to watch our clothes coming out of the wringer in a long flat strip, recognizable yet unfamiliar when blended and compressed. The clean soap smell and the bleach used for whites were sharp in my nose. She was very fond of bleach and occasionally coloured garments would have pale spots where they had encountered drops of bleach not meant for them. A clothesline stretched from our back porch to a post at the end of the garden, and for my mother a day was perfect when a load of washing could dry outside and be brought in crisp and smelling like air and sunshine. She claimed to love ironing and I clearly remember the smell of the steam iron pressing cotton. Each item was ironed, from underwear to face cloths. She sewed clothes for us, too—every Easter Rosamond and I would have new matching dresses of the same material in different colours.

In spite of the changes of direction and the challenges in my mother's young adult life, I believe she was content and fulfilled in her role as a Canadian wife and mother. Her marriage was happy, she had family support, I was on the road to health and Rosamond gave no cause for concern. It had become the sort of life she would have been raised to expect and strive for. Having lived through my illness, I feel she became more relaxed in her obsession with germs and safety. In her view, western germs didn't hold the terror of those in India.

4

Lourdes

My stubborn and independent nature led to considerable conflict with my mother. She was a fierce disciplinarian and would rise even taller than her five foot nine inches to say, "You'll do what I say because I say so!" and "You absolutely can't wear that! It reflects on *me*!" There was never any room for compromise. As my mother told it, I always chose the opposite to what she wanted. I saw it the other way round. On one famous occasion my mother—the family barber—decided I needed a haircut. I wanted to grow my hair, and I refused to let her near me with her scissors, screaming and hollering and covering my head with a dishtowel. I won that battle.

Because of the importance she put on appearances, it must have been a challenge for her to accept my physical form; as I grew, not only could I not walk, but I developed a fairly severe curvature of the spine. More than once she told us a story from her school days: "When I was at school in England there was a classmate with a hunchback. A perfectly nice girl, but the other girls would taunt her. I never was unkind to her, but neither would I be her friend. I was only eleven or twelve, but it still upsets me to think of how I behaved towards her. I have never forgotten."

After leaving the hospital I had been fitted for a set of leg braces I had to be buckled and laced into. For an hour each day, I would faithfully inch my way, using crutches, around and around the carpet in the living room. I was very slow and easily toppled over. I couldn't negotiate even a half-inch step on my own, so it was useless as a means for getting around, but I did enjoy the added height that standing gave me.

Both of my parents were very keen on getting me to walk again.

Strangers would approach my mother and me, asking in simpering voices, their heads tilted to one side, "Will she ever walk again?" She would answer fiercely, "Of *course* she will walk again!" There were blessings conducted by priests, anointments with holy oil and holy water, and once a Pentecostal faith healer who grabbed and shook my feet and legs and prayed loudly "Heal this child, Lord! Heal this child!" And then, "It's a miracle! She's moving her foot! Life is returning! Praise the Lord!" My parents had neglected to let the fellow know that I could wiggle my right toes.

When I was seven, the family started saving to send me with my mother to Lourdes. As the story went, in 1858 the Virgin Mary appeared eighteen times to a 14-year-old village girl by the name of Bernadette Soubirous and instructed her to dig in a grotto where a spring would appear. The water was said to have miraculous healing powers. My family was not Catholic, but I guess they wanted to cover all the bases. My mother and father gave up smoking cigarettes and put the money away. On top of the fridge was a tin with the label "Lourdes Fund." Friends and other family members chipped in.

Just before my eighth birthday, my mother and I boarded the train in Vancouver for Quebec City. From there, we boarded an ocean liner, for the eight-day journey across the Atlantic to Le Havre, France. On our arrival we took a ferry across the English Channel, and we spent several weeks visiting family friends before crossing the water again to connect with the pilgrimage train to Lourdes.

The train was filled with people on stretchers, in wheelchairs, on canes and crutches. Many of them were elderly, accompanied by nurses or nuns. I was the only child. As we rode through France people stood at their back garden fences watching and waving. Especially moving was the singing of "Ave Maria" by the people on the train and those lining the tracks as we approached Lourdes, in the picturesque Pyrenees Mountains.

The towering Basilica at Lourdes was flanked by twin ramped arms leading from the Rosary Square, which could hold nearly 80,000 people, up to the Basilica itself. One of the ramps overlooked a winding river and pasture, and we could see beyond to wooded hillsides. Thousands of people attended the masses in Rosary Square—processions of women, their hair covered by white gauze kerchiefs; priests looking important, robed in white, red or black cassocks; stretchers on wheels with their immobile cargo and people in all types of 1940's and 50's style European wheelchairs, pushed by bustling helpers, everyone clutching rosaries.

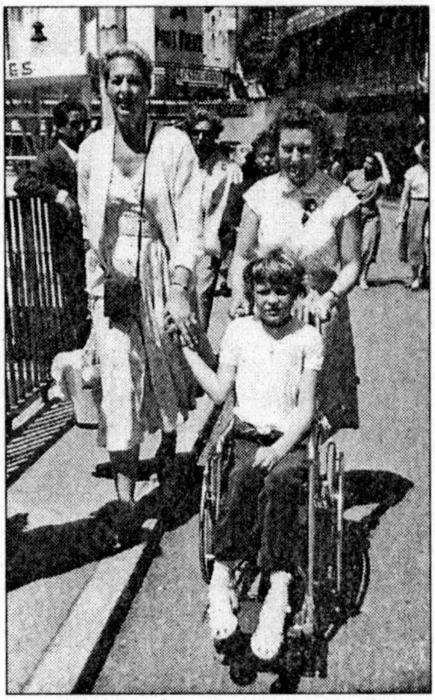

Mary and Judy in Lourdes.

My mother and I stayed in a hotel, where I celebrated my eighth birthday. I was presented with a strange, pistachio-coloured birthday cake made of ice cream, unlike anything I had ever eaten. Gilou, a young French medical student-volunteer, was assigned to push me around the hilly town for sight seeing and souvenir shopping. He was incredibly handsome, and I developed an enormous crush on him.

Each day grey-robed nuns, their sleeves rolled up, would totally immerse me in the stone baths of very cold spring water. It was fun, and not at all holy-seeming to an eight-year-old. The possibility of a miracle did not concern me. I was more interested in looking at the other naked people waiting for their turn in the baths. I was fascinated to see that grey hair on the head could mean grey pubic hair, or even no pubic hair. One morning the nuns convinced my mother to have a dip in the holy water. Somewhat reluctantly she removed her clothes and was lifted off her feet and into the tank by four strong nuns. I never felt there was any expectation, from my mother, for a miracle, or disappointment that there wasn't one.

On our return sea voyage, I made a friend my age. We spent our time going back and forth between ordinary class, where we were travelling, to the first-class lounge and games room, where we pretended we belonged. I made my singing debut with the Italian ship's orchestra, a quintet, singing "Que Sera, Sera" and "He's Got the Whole World in His Hands." My performance kindled a lust for an audience I would never lose.

5

conflicts

AT THE AGE OF THIRTEEN, I had a friend from school over to visit, and I showed her what I could do with my crutches and braces. She said, "Oh, you look funny, your bum sticks out!" That was the last time I put on the braces. My wheelchair was a far more graceful and useful way of getting about.

In spite of all the energy they put into hoping I would walk, my mother and father never treated me as disabled. Perhaps some of my mother's fierce discipline with her children (particularly, I felt, with me) came from fear of pandering and spoiling me; pity was not allowed. She told me that I was never cuddly, even as a small child. I had sharp elbows, and I used them. Independence was always a large part of my nature.

My mother had very strong opinions about how and when things should be done. From her, I had to endure some fashion restrictions I considered unfair. A pair of black, thick-heeled, lace-up granny shoes, (the rage when I was a teenager), that I found at St. Vincent de Paul thrift store horrified and disgusted my mother. "You absolutely *cannot* wear those shoes! They look dreadful, and who knows where they might have come from!" I did persist in wearing them.

I had always wanted to climb, and roofs in particular appealed to me. As a small child, I had longed to climb up the ladder onto the roof of our back shed. In PE class in elementary school, I had one day on the jungle gym. It was exciting to pull myself onto a higher rung and then a higher one; I was a monkey. I didn't get to the top, though, because gym class was only half an hour long. Sadly, by the next time the jungle gym had been put away.

During my teens, our family moved to a flat-roofed bungalow in West Vancouver. My friend Janet was visiting one day, and as we were exploring behind the carport we came upon the ladder used for getting onto the roof to clear leaves or snow. It was a beautiful warm October day and we came up with a plan. I climbed onto the first rung and then, with Janet pushing from below and me pulling myself up rung by rung, I made it onto the roof. I was on top of the world! My heart pounded with excitement and with the knowledge that I had done something forbidden by my ever-worrying mother. We had a panoramic view from the roof: Burrard Inlet, the Lions Gate Bridge, the freighters waiting their turn to enter the harbour and unload their cargo, the trees down the hillside splendid in their autumn colours. After gazing our fill, we descended the ladder. I, of course, had to tell my family of my accomplishment. My father was delighted, my mother furious.

My mother and I often had stormy clashes. During dinner one evening, my mother and I had a terrible fight. Rosamond and I were in the kitchen, doing the dishes, while my mother sat in the living room bewailing her life with me. "We had to give up so much and leave our life in India because of you! Oh, the times I sat up through the night with you when you were ill! And every day I had to push you to school, through the rain and the snow, and then walk all the way back again to fetch you. And you are so ungrateful. Whatever did I do to deserve this?" The heat built in my brain like a volcano, and I suddenly opened my mouth and started to shriek at the top of my lungs—three or four blood-curdling screams, and then over and over again: "She's going to kill me! She's going to kill me! She's going to kill me!" I gave in completely to hysteria until Rosamond rushed me outside and up the steep driveway into the back lane. I remained outside until my breathing had calmed somewhat, then returned to the house and shut myself in my room. Before going to bed my mother opened my door and said coldly, "Do you have anything to say to me?" I replied in an equally cool voice, "No." Nothing more was spoken of the outburst.

The conflicts with my mother were tempered briefly by the fortunate arrival of a baby sister, Amanda. In the early days of their marriage, my parents talked about having four children. My polio and their having to move back to Canada and start from scratch financially had delayed those dreams. But Dad had a good job now, and I no longer needed special care. Amanda was an important part of my teenage years, and feeding, bathing, dressing and playing with her gave me complete confidence in my own future parenting skills.

I had a steady boyfriend from the age of fourteen, which helped to smooth some of the rough paths of teenage-hood. At seventeen, I got my driver's license and my mother had hand controls installed in her new car and generously allowed me to drive it.

In spite of the difficulties with my mother, I think the fact that I had a boyfriend and a driver's license, gave her comfort. I was a regular teenager, almost ready to move away from home and make my own way. She had done her job.

6

grown up

AFTER GRADUATING from high school, I attended the University of British Columbia for one year. I went because it was expected of me, and that's what my friends were doing. But flower power was all around me, and I was a true child of the 60's. Travel and music were what interested me.

I moved into a large communal house with five friends, bought a guitar and continued to sing. We had parties, shared gourmet dinners, and listened to music: rock and roll, folk, Indian music. Philosophy and intensity and laughter filled the air. Always there was talk of travel, and of moving back to the land, out of the city. One of my housemates became my boyfriend and we moved to a small hand-built cabin on the Sunshine Coast of British Columbia. After three years, he moved on, but I lived there for seven years, my isolation relieved by trips to Oregon, California and other parts of BC. I acquired my beloved Appalachian Mountain dulcimer, an American instrument with drone strings that makes a sitar-like sound. I started to write the occasional song. Hitchhiking was my main means of transportation, and I had hand-controls installed in a friend's car so that we could share the driving on southern road trips.

I'd been living in the cabin with Ben, a Swiss artist, for two years. In the spring of 1977, I discovered happily that I was pregnant. Doctors had always told me that pregnancy would mean a Cesarean delivery due to my small, distorted pelvis, but my gynecologist believed a natural delivery might be possible. My labour was about 6 hours long before pushing. After I'd pushed for two and a half hours, the doctor assisted the delivery with forceps and a large episiotomy, but Eliza did travel down the birth canal. She was a perfect tiny baby, 5 pounds, 13 ounces.

When Eliza was just over a year old, Ben and I married and bought a house on a small piece of land on Vancouver Island with the help of a down payment from my parents. We kept goats, chickens and ducks and worked a large organic vegetable garden. Six years later our daughter, Belinda, was born. I continued to sing and play guitar and dulcimer at local folk events, daycare centres and restaurants. When Belinda was four and Eliza eleven, Ben decided that family life was not something he could handle, but I stayed on with the children.

My mother often said that she never wanted to go back to India because it wouldn't be the same, and she wanted to remember Mirzapur as it was when she left it. During the time I was pregnant with Eliza, my father had made a return visit to India. After retiring from his years as an industrial first-aid attendant, he had graduated from the University of British Columbia with a degree in Asian studies, and he travelled to India overland from Europe through the Middle East, just like any young backpacker. He was received at his old home in the Mirzapur district, like a beloved long-absent relative. My father's stories of his travels kindled a dormant desire to make my own way back to the land of my beginnings.

India had been a big part of my years growing up in Canada: pet Hindustani words and phrases used by my family, the stories my parents told about our life there, the wonderful curries my father had learned to make from our Indian cook, Ghulam, and the carpets, bedspreads and jewelry in our house. As an adult, I would cry during movie or television scenes that took place in India, sometimes sobbing uncontrollably. I had a distinct memory of becoming another person after having polio. I was still me, but a new me had been created. I vaguely remember a few details of my illness: I was tired, my left leg collapsed on the way to the bathroom, and then I was in a bed in the Landour community hospital. I'd forgotten the pain of having a syringe inserted into my spinal chord, to take a diagnostic sample, but I knew my father had told me the story of The Three Bears during the procedure, and he said it was one of the worst experiences of his life. I did remember the itching. "Daddy, I have an itch right beside my nose." My father covered his finger with his handkerchief and rubbed to the left of my nose. "No. Closer to my nose, please." "Is that better, darling?" "Ah, yes, that's it." And there was my beloved Dukharan, standing framed in the doorway, not allowed to come closer for fear of infection. After coming down with polio, I would only converse in English, even with Dukharan, with whom I normally spoke only Mirzapur dialect Hindi. Perhaps my child's brain, closely tied to my mother, somehow associated English with safety. Whatever the case, the girl in India was the child who had stayed behind, and I always missed her. It would be more than forty years before I would go to find her again.

7

preparations

IN THE YEARS following my divorce, the idea of going back to India grew ever stronger and I started making plans. Eliza had moved to the city when she was eighteen. I felt Belinda was a perfect age to take traveling. I spent two years planning our journey.

"Ross, will you come to India with me? One way or another I am going." Ross, my friend and roommate, agreed to be our travelling companion. I had been saving money, so I booked our tickets to New Delhi for November 18, 1996.

Before my father came back to Canada, he trained a replacement, Geoffrey Seager, to take over his position in the carpet firm. He and Geoffrey had become great friends, and in addition to years of correspondence, my father stayed with him when he went back to Mirzapur. I wrote to Geoffrey telling him of our plans and asking if we could stay at his bungalow when we came to India. My father had had cancer for several years. Shortly before he died in November 1995, I received word from Geoffrey. He wrote a very welcoming letter saying how much he and his wife, Kusum were looking forward to our visit. It gave my father great pleasure and peace of mind to know we would be well looked after.

After my father's death, my mother reminded me of two paintings Dad had bought for me in India while we lived there, as an investment to assist with my university education. In my research, I found that the work of the artist, Jamini Roy, was fetching a decent price at auctions. Sotheby's sold them in London as part of an India auction and they went for more than I'd expected, very helpful for my trip.

In the weeks leading up to our departure date, my life took on an air of unreality. I was really going to India, back to Mirzapur. What would it be like to see it all again?

We planned on a stay of three and a half months. Belinda was keen on the idea of going but was too young to really imagine how it might be. Ross had travelled extensively in Mexico and Central America, but not Asia. And I had lived there only as an overly protected and privileged white child. We planned to travel not only to Mirzapur and my birthplace, Mussoorie, but to many other places we had read about: the Rajasthani desert, Goa on the west coast, Kerala and Karnataka in the south. The biggest question for me was how I would manage to make my way through India with a wheelchair. Would the three of us be up to the challenge?

We sublet our house so that the cats would have a caretaker and the mortgage would be paid. We packed and repacked our bags, eliminating, adding and reshuffling things. We read articles and books about India, and scheduled dinners and visits with friends who'd been there. We decided Belinda would be the one to piggyback me onto trains and buses; she was big for her twelve years and very strong, and Ross's back was not too good. We did some practicing around the house and the back yard to get into shape.

Finally, after the months of preparation, the time had come. Our journey was beginning!

8

return to mirzapur

THE FIRST SMELL OF DELHI was a burned rubber smell, with nothing familiar about it. I would later learn that this was the pervading smell of the city, pollution on a scale I could never have imagined. It stung our eyes and frequently made us hold handkerchiefs and scarves over our noses.

A friend of ours who worked in North India as a guide for a few months each year had arranged for us to be met at the airport and to be taxied to our hotel. The drive into Delhi was like some insane Mad Magazine cartoon, with cars, auto rickshaws, motorcycles, scooters, bicycles, buses, trucks and pedestrians forming a giant roiling river of traffic. All of the vehicles honked their horns all the time, for no reason that I could see. To our eyes, there seemed to be no apparent order, vehicles filled up every available space, moving along crazily like bumper cars. Obviously they sometimes bumped each other, as evidenced by the scratches, dents and lack of side mirrors.

We were woken in our hotel room at 4:00 in the morning by drumming and wild chanting that got faster and faster until it reached a positive frenzy. It finished after a time but was replaced by chanting. The hotel was next door to a large Sikh Gurdwara temple, we'd later learn. In the morning after breakfast, Belinda and I headed out onto the street. She convinced me we should take a tuc-tuc, one of the little auto rickshaws we saw everywhere. It was easy for me to get into, and there was plenty of room for Belinda and me and my folded wheelchair. Our driver was Suresh, a very interesting professional guide. As we motored along in the midst of all different sorts of conveyances, I suddenly burst out "Hathi!" Ambling up the road was an elephant. Without thinking, I'd said the first word that came to my lips. It was my four-year-old Hindustani-speaking child who had exclaimed.

On our second morning, Suresh took the three of us to Old Delhi, where we had our first experience with begging children. Our tuc-tuc was instantly surrounded by a small group of them, very young, very poor who plucked at us and pleaded with desperate faces. A baby, held by its thin older sister was covered with sores. Suresh had told us not to show any money while we were in Old Delhi. He gave them some rupees, but told us it was best to give food or chocolate, as the money went to the parents. Of the group, he said, "I know this family, their parents drink." We were overwhelmed by the plight of these children, and Belinda was in tears.

Our day-long trip with Suresh took us to the Gandhi Memorial, India Gate and government buildings. All the while he entertained us with stories of Indian history, politics, his family and his job as a tuc-tuc driver.

Our train to Mirzapur was scheduled to leave at 8:00 PM from the New Delhi station on our third day in the city. At 7:00 PM a taxi plus an assistant from the travel agent picked us up at our hotel. Innocents that we were, we didn't realize one hour was not really sufficient time to drive to the station, find the platform, locate the train and get on, not to mention finding our seats.

When we arrived at the station, our travel agent man seemed a bit confused about where to go. A porter checked our tickets and whisked me away in my chair after sending Ross and Belinda up the stairs to the overhead walkway to find the correct platform. The porter raced with me down to the end of the platform and across the tracks where the carts and barrows cross. He was running, running, shouting for people to move, both of us pushing people and things out of our path. "Side, side, side!" he called out over and over. So many people. Crowds and crowds of them. It was soon after Diwali, the festival of lights, and people were returning from travels all over India to visit their families.

We raced along side of the train, and there in the crowds pressing up against it, appeared the white, worried faces of Ross and Belinda, who had been wondering if they would ever see me again. Ross went to find our seats. He discovered we only had two confirmed berths, and they were not together. We jammed onto the train, me on Belinda's back, and the two of us sat down as close as we could get to one of our reserved spots, in someone else's seat. I was on the edge of panic and claustrophobia—we were booked on an air-conditioned sleeper car, but the air conditioning is not on until the train starts moving, and the sealed windows allow no airflow.

I struggled to suppress my verging hysteria. Belinda and I squashed together in the narrow berth, our heads at opposite ends, trying to find some degree of comfort. She slept while I worried the conductor would come along and make us move. He never did, though and I hoped whoever's spot we had was in the place reserved for us. Indian people are very accommodating, we would discover. More than once in our train journeys I was sure we were in the wrong seats, but we were never made to feel that we were putting anyone out.

No sleep for me that night. All I could think was, I am going home to Mirzapur, I am going back home to Mirzapur. The conductor came by to speak to some other passengers, and I heard the phrase "Canadian family" a couple of times. I wept as I heard the young mother across from me talking to her small children in the phrases so familiar between mother and child, though I couldn't understand the words. The four-year-old Judy would have had no such incomprehension. She would have wondered what all the fuss was about. Just another train journey. Fun, yes, exciting, yes, but let's just settle down for the night and get on with it, shall we?

We got our belongings arranged early in the morning so we could disembark quickly; Geoffrey had told us the train didn't stop long at Mirzapur. The train slowed, and there in front of me was the Mirzapur railway station, a sight I hadn't consciously remembered, but one that I knew so very well when I saw it. I burst into floods of tears. Forty-three years before, in the month of May, I had left this railway station with my mother, father and baby sister, Rosamond, our things packed for another journey to the hills to escape the hot weather, a trip thousands of Europeans had made over the last century or more. There had been no foreshadowing of the events to come, no hint that our family's comfortable way of life was to end with such drama and heartache.

Kusum had spent the night in Mirzapur to celebrate a Sikh occasion and so was the one to meet us at the station. She was a lovely woman with a rich, throaty voice, very pleasant to listen to. She greeted us warmly, as I continued to weep, and told me my Aunt Rosamond, my father's older sister, had reacted in exactly the same way when returning to India after many years. A jeep and driver was ready to take us on the forty-five minute trip to Raipuri, where Geoffrey was waiting.

I was in tears for half of the journey. The mud huts, the buffalo, the men and boys on their big, black Hero bicycles, the ekkas, the bullock carts, the fields, the pi-dogs. All of them so familiar, but up to that point, forgotten—mango trees and banyan trees, small happy children, cows, goats, piles of dried cow dung ready to be used for cooking fires. The recognition I felt for these scenes was shocking and profound.

Our jeep driver hurtled down the road, swerving to avoid cars, trucks, bicycles and rickshaws. I had calmed myself considerably by the time we arrived at Raipuri at about 7:00 AM, and there was Geoffrey to meet us, wearing his morning lungi (a wrap around sarong worn by men). My mother and sisters had visited with Geoffrey during summer visits to England, and I was the only member of my family who had not yet met him, although we had written several times and spoken on the phone. He was kind and gracious, with an amused twinkle in his eye. His mannerisms and expressions reminded me of my dad. The same British Indian influences, no doubt. Geoffrey had made his home in India for forty-three years, with yearly visits to England to see his grown-up children and grandchildren.

After breakfast came a very welcome bath and a nap. I didn't know then that the Raipuri bathtub was the last tub I would see for the next three and a half months. The house at Raipuri was grand: marble floors and staircase, beautiful carpets and many large bronze statues of Hindu deities—dancing Ganesh, dancing Siva, Krishna and Lakshmi. The house looked out on a beautifully kept lawn and flower gardens with red, magenta and cream Bougainvillea framing the screened verandah where we had breakfast and lunch served to us by Ram Lal and Punoo, two of the five house staff. Dinner was a more formal affair, served in the dining room, with Ram Lal and Punoo constantly coming by to refill our plates.

Nine servants—five indoor staff, one mali, one chowkidar, and two drivers—would seem to indicate a life of leisure for the householders. But managing that many people, doing all the marketing and the meal planning and taking care of house guests is a full time occupation for Kusum. Geoffrey is a partner in the Raipuri Carpet Company Ltd., and so every winter plays host to many carpet buyers from all over the world. And a more gracious host and hostess one could never find.

In the Mirzapur district, much of the Indian lifestyle my parents experienced would have been similar to what we were seeing, except for the vast increase in the population. The life of Europeans in India at the tail end of the Raj was not so different from that of the well-to-do Indians and Europeans who live in India today. It seemed that except for those who were very poor, most families had at least one hired person to help with cleaning and cooking.

The contrast between the Raipuri house and compound and the surrounding village and countryside was immense. As we walked through Geoffrey and Kusum's gate out onto the street, we entered another world—one that in many ways has been unchanged for hundreds of years. Mirzapur was an agricultural area and much of the farming was done with animals to pull the plough along with the occasional tractor. People's houses were built of mud, cow dung and some locally made brick, and their cooking fuel was dried cow dung. With the exception of petrol and some very intermittent electricity, the lives and beliefs of the villagers had remained the same for hundreds, even thousands of years.

The homes we saw, some under giant spreading mango or banyan trees, usually had one or two water buffalo tethered in front, animals used for milk and dung. Small children played about, and sometimes an old man would be sleeping on a charpoy, a wood-framed, string-woven cot. The surrounding fields were filled with bright yellow mustard, used for cooking oil, as well as lentils, millet, and sugar cane.

Geoffrey told us that most of the cottages in Raipuri and the surrounding villages had a room with one or two looms for carpet weaving. We visited one across the road from the bungalow. It was common to see people on bicycles, scooters, or in ekkas taking rolled-up carpets to the factory to be trimmed, finished and prepared for export. Men do the weaving, with fathers teaching their sons. According to Geoffrey, though, there were no children working in the district's many carpet factories. When a German magazine crew came to Raipuri to do research on bonded child labour, he took them everywhere they asked to go and in the week they were there, they found nothing. There were other places in India where children were essentially sold into slavery to work off a parent's debt, we knew, but not in Mirzapur.

We observed several tree schools on our trips around the district. These were usually two classes of children sitting in the dust, in the shade of a large tree, with two blackboards and two teachers. They learned basic reading and writing, and we heard them counting in English. There were many, many children in the area; on one of our walks, we counted forty children walking with us along one short bit of road. Kusum's sister, Moti, was a gynecologist who taught family planning and basic health care to the tribal people in the foothills of the Himalayas, and on some of her visits to Raipuri she worked with local villagers. Family planning is not a popular concept, Kusum told us. Men believe vasectomies will diminish their virility and the women believe tubal ligation will make them sick

One afternoon Kusum took us to a lady's sing-song, a pre-wedding party for a bride and all her female friends and relatives. The women gathered in a hall with padded mats on the floor for the guests to sit upon, while the men waited on chairs in the lobby. Songs were sung, one after another. Kusum performed a very funny number, pantomiming with a shawl about her head, portraying a drunken or stoned character, and everyone joined in. The girls and women were beautifully dressed in bold colour combinations, fuchsias with orange and green, reds and pinks with yellow and turquoise. Usually a lady's sing-song also involves mehndi (hand and foot decoration done with henna). Since this wedding would take place in another state in a month's time, the mehndi would be done closer to the wedding day. Belinda sat and observed and I chatted with several ladies including one Mrs. Sharma who had known my mother. A traditional dance performance followed the songs and visiting and then came the food. By this time the men had joined the festivities, and the bride's father was insistent that Ross and Belinda and I eat. A little delicate due to side effects from my anti-malarial medication, I only nibbled, but Ross ate heartily, and Belinda consumed some lurid-looking sweets.

We accompanied Kusum later that week, when she went to take a gift and pay her respects to another bride, the daughter of an upper-caste Thakur family. The bride was weeping as she received Kusum's gift of money. Thakurs are traditionally landowners, and they consider it beneath them to work the soil. This impoverished family were supporting themselves by selling off bits of their land. Their two-hundred-year-old house was rundown and dark—an amazing crumbling structure.

9

back to bisunderpur

UNTIL ONLY TEN YEARS BEFORE, this E. Hill & Company bungalow, had continued to house employees. Kusum made arrangements by telephone with the company for us to visit my family's old bungalow at Bisunderpur, across the Ganges River, not far from Mirzapur. He also arranged for us to meet Laloo, the young servant who had worked for us during our last year in India, and Suleiman, who had been our sweeper. It was, as usual, a beautiful, warm day when we set out after lunch. Geoffrey, Kusum, Ross, Belinda, and I piled into the jeep and drove through the villages and Mirzapur city, along the Ganges to Bisunderpur village. The watchman was waiting for us at the gate between the brick wall at the end of the dirt driveway. There had been no such wall or gate when our family lived there. At the front of the bungalow we stopped. Almost immediately came Laloo, having taken a fairly long bus ride from the E. Hill & Company Khamariah bungalow, across the river, where he was employed. He had a tall, slender frame, and was dressed in a uniform of a white Nehru jacket and trousers. He reached out to shyly grasp my hands in both of his, tears running down our faces, wetting our huge smiles. He had high cheekbones, a neatly trimmed grey mustache, a receding hairline and milk-coffee coloured skin. "Ah, Judy Baba! Aap kaisi hain?" He had been a nineteen-year-old boy when we left India and now he was past sixty. I spoke very little Hindi and he spoke very little English but we communicated well with Kusum acting as our translator.

The beautiful two hundred year old building had fallen into decay. It was never made clear to me just why the roof was never repaired, and why the company allowed its condition to deteriorate. I believe company politics were involved.

Here was the stately house my mother had lived in and loved. The bungalow looked familiar on the outside, but smaller than I remembered. We walked all around it, through the weeds that grew where there had once been lawn, over the thick layer of fallen leaves from trees that had grown up on both sides of the house, while we waited for our driver to fetch the keys from the company office close by. Bougainvillea covered the front verandah and hung low to the ground. Four palm trees stood on the grassy area surrounded by the circular driveway. A small pile of possessions and sleeping mats belonging to the chowkidars, the bungalow's night and day watchmen, were arranged on the verandah close to one of the doors.

Suleiman arrived, as we strolled the grounds, to more tearful greetings. He was a very distinguished gentleman with a neatly trimmed white beard, a spotless white long shirt and trousers and a crisp white Nehru cap. He worked close by, for Edward Oakley, another carpet man, caring for Edward's two dogs. It was a pleasant retirement occupation, and Edward called him, Suleiman the Magnificent, as we would later learn.

Two large bunches of keys were produced by the driver and handed over to one of the chowkidars and I waited excitedly as each key was tried at every locked door. Not one would open. I could feel my heart beating as I struggled to remain calm. The second chowkidar tried all the keys at each door. Were we to come all this way and not be able to step into the vast bungalow, into my past? Our quiet jeep driver, who had been observing the procedure, asked if he could try. He tried one bungalow door with the key to the jeep, and sure enough, it opened. How typically Indian, I thought. Out of seeming anarchy, things work in odd and unexpected ways.

We stepped over the threshold into rooms with high, water-stained walls and dark rotted woodwork. Was this really my first home? Was this where I had learned to crawl, to walk and to run about? Was it within these walls where I had chattered away in Hindustani to the servants, where my first English words had so charmed my parents? The roof had collapsed in places, allowing the monsoon rains to pour in. The photos

The bungalow in ruins. (photos by Ross Hunt)

I'd seen in my parents' family albums, of spacious elegance and bright cream walls, bore no resemblance to this completely ruined interior. Going from room to room, on Belinda's back, I tried to remember how it had once been. Outside the bungalow, it was easier. I imagined myself here as a small child, running in my pink rubber boots through the water-soaked lawns with Dukharan and Chipso, our dog—the beautiful old white-washed bungalow on one side, the Ganges River on the other, in between the lawn, emerald green in the monsoon season, and the carefully tended gardens. It's a blessing that my mother can't see this, I thought. It would break her heart.

Laloo insisted on pushing my chair everywhere we went. "I pushed you in your pram as a baby along this driveway, and I am so happy to be pushing you still!" he said as Kusum translated. He must have been confusing me with Rosamond—I was past the pram stage when Laloo came to work for our family—but I was touched by his memory.

"Belinda walks just like Norbury Sahib!" Suleiman exclaimed. Ross and I laughed. Our whole family had always said Belinda walked just like my dad.

As my mother had written, my dad had once told the local grave-digger, "When I die, old man, it is my wish that I be burned and cast into the Mother Ganges." Now was my chance to make his wish come true. Our group walked through the village of Bisunderpur winding our way through narrow passageways past small homes, tethered goats and staring children, to the riverbank. The bank was too steep to make the water easily accessible for me, so Kusum and I stayed up top as the others walked down to the river, and climbed aboard a boat Laloo had arranged for a short trip to scatter some of my father's ashes. I knew that he would have been delighted with the whole procedure. For twenty-three years, Mirzapur had been his home, and he deeply loved India and its people. This was a fitting place to cast his ashes, and a fitting manner in which to do it—by a beloved granddaughter and two old and faithful servants. His ashes would float down the river and on to Benares, to mix with those of others at that most holy of Hindu places.

A very old woman wrapped in a red print sari was squatting close to Kusum and me. She watched the events with interest. Kusum told her who I was and what we were doing. She looked at me, and then looked back to the scene on the river, and then turned to Kusum and said she remembered well the Sahib and Memsahib; they had been very kind to the villagers.

When the group returned from the river, we walked back along the road to the Mirzapur Club, a gathering place for carpet people in the neighbourhood. The club has been going for at least a hundred years and it boasts that it has never been segregated.

We ordered fish and chips, with Indian ketchup, and watched the sun set over the Ganges. I knew that Dukharan, my special friend and favourite servant had died many years before but had been hoping to meet Dasrath, his youngest son, with whom I'd played as a child. Distressingly, I learned from Laloo that Dasrath had been murdered by poison the previous year, seemingly over a land dispute.

After dinner Ross and I walked into the village to buy a bar of soap. Word had spread quickly through Bisunderpur about our visit, and the ancient shopkeeper spoke with great warmth about my parents.

As we rumbled along in the jeep, to Raipuri, I was quiet as I reflected on the day that had brought me full circle back to my first home, and to Laloo and Suleiman, old friends who thought they would never see me again. Judy Baba had come back.

10

Visiting

KUSUM, WHO WAS a superb behind the scenes organizer, thoughtfully planned rest days between visiting days. As everything was so new and strange, we were all thankful for those unscheduled days when we would read and nap and go for walks.

Our next visit was to Khamariah, a half hour jeep drive from Raipuri. It also belonged to E. Hill & Company and had been the home of great friends of my parents, Bill and Bimla Wallace and their daughters, Lila and Tara. I'd spent much time there as a child. This bungalow and gardens were beautifully kept and maintained. The residents were away, so we couldn't go inside, but we were able to visit the grounds and gardens, where we met Laloo and his wife and children and grandchildren. Laloo works as part of the staff at the Khamariah bungalow. He and his wife gave us gifts: a lovely red and green shawl for me, a lungi for Ross (it became one of his most useful garments on our trip, serving as a sheet, a towel, a pillow case, as well as a lungi) and a box of pastries for Belinda. Such generosity from people who have little.

Geoffrey's friend, Dr. Rajan, who lives in the village of Khamariah, invited us for lunch, and our visit to his house was the highlight of Belinda's trip. The family owned a pet monkey called Rishma, who completely took to her. All afternoon Rishma sat on Belinda's shoulder and picked through her hair and ears, grooming her and looking for lice. The monkey and Belinda were both upset when we had to leave; Rishma cried and chattered and jumped up and down the pole to which she was chained. Dr. Rajan promised that when we returned to Raipuri after our travels in the rest of India, Belinda could come and spend the night. She talked constantly about the invitation from then on.

After being at Raipuri for a week we made a day trip to Allahabad to visit Kuldip, an old friend of my father's. Dad had hired Kuldip as the engineer to build the chimney at the Khamariah carpet factory some fifty years before.

Allahabad was an hour and a half from Raipuri down the famous Grand Trunk Road, an ancient route with much history to tell along its way. The road runs from Calcutta on the east coast of India through Delhi, Amritsar in the Punjab, into Lahore and Peshawar in Pakistan and on to Kabul, Afghanistan, a distance of about 2600 kilometers. It was built under the leadership of Sher Shah Suri, a sixteenth century ruler of northern India, to link the remote provinces of his huge empire. In some places the road reestablished routes that had existed since the time of the Maurya Empire, from 325 BC to 183 BC. This ancient dynasty had brought nearly all of India, including Afghanistan, under one rule for the first time. Alexander the Great's armies used the route to invade northern India. Rudyard Kipling, who set much of his story "Kim" along the Grand Trunk Road, called it "such a river of life as exists nowhere else in the world".

The modern Grand Trunk Road, however, is a route best avoided as we soon discovered. Down the centre of the highway, really only a single lane's width, roared huge orange transport trucks, called lorries, made by TATA, India's largest steel company which was started in 1907. These lorries were decorated with garlands of marigolds and tinsel, pictures of deities, and signs saying "KING OF THE ROAD" and "HONK YOUR HORN." Playing chicken and drunkenness were common among the lorry drivers, and the evidence of previous crashes littered the road. We passed one fresh accident, from which people were pulling the bloodied, dead body of the driver. I turned my head away after the briefest glance, but Ross and Belinda took a good look, and Belinda became white-faced and quiet. To distract her, Kusum told Belinda a grisly story about a murder along that same stretch of road and some tales about one of the Hindu gods.

We had the nearest of misses ourselves along the bridge into Allahabad over the Sangam, where the Ganges and Yamuna rivers meet. A jeep sped towards us head on until during the last fraction of a second the driver suddenly saw us and swerved. It was a rather shaken group who arrived at Mr. and Mrs. Kuldip's house.

Mrs. Kuldip, a sweet old lady with snow-white hair and a round cheery face, had prepared tea, coffee and biscuits for us at a small table with an embroidered cloth set up in their modest courtyard. Kuldip, as my father always called him, was a tall, wiry figure dressed in a suit and white shirt. He sported a conical fake-fur Russian-style hat. His sincere smile and bright clever eyes lit up his face. Our visit was filled with warm sentiment, since both of the Kuldips attributed the success of their entire family to the fact that my father had hired Kuldip for the engineering job at the Khamariah carpet factory so many years before. The Kuldips' children are professionals now, their daughter a doctor. At eighty-four, Kuldip still rode around Allahabad on his scooter, sometimes with Mrs. Kuldip perched sidesaddle on the back. The ride back to Raipuri was without mishap, although we were all a little tense.

One of the lovely things about our stay with Geoffrey and Kusum was that Belinda and the servants enjoyed each other so much. Ram Lal and Punoo called her "baby." Krishna, who did laundry, sweeping and other household chores, was amused by Belinda, though she thought her very untidy, and was particularly dismayed by the dirtiness of Belinda's socks. At thirty-four, Krishna was mother of two grown children and already a grandmother. Another servant, Dilari was grandmother to eleven-year-old Rita, who was starting her life as a servant at Raipuri as well. Rita was mostly a helper for her grandmother, and her family's biggest concern was getting her married. Children in the villages married very young but didn't go to live with the husband's family until they were about sixteen. Rita and Belinda played for hours. "*Chelo, chelo*, Belinda. Come on!" Rita would call from the garden with her ball, laughing and running as she encouraged Belinda to join her. Rita taught Belinda to play a form of jacks with stones, and it was she who showed Belinda how to drape the sari she had bought for herself in Delhi.

Belinda borrowed a bicycle from the household gardener and cycled to Ram Lal's house to have her feet painted by his wife. The women in the village painted their feet with a bright magenta dye, all around the sides and between the toes. It wasn't fine work like the mehndi designs, but done with broad strokes and large circles. Ross and I strolled up the road after a while to see how things were going, and all we could see was a large crowd of people, mostly women and children. In the middle of the crowd sat Belinda, having her feet painted. It was a wonderful sight.

11

Mussoorie

DEHRA DUN, where I was born, was the closest railway stop to Mussoorie, where we'd spent time during the hot weather and where I'd contracted polio. Belinda and Ross and I had an invitation from Kusum's sister, Moti, who lived in Dehra Dun, to stay with her. From there we would visit the hill town.

With fond farewells to the Raipuri household and a promise to return in three months' time, we set off along the Grand Trunk road to Varanasi, for a train back to Delhi. It was only our second train trip, and we hadn't learned much from our confused and frantic first railway experience. We hired porters to help me and the bags get up the stairs, then down the stairs to the correct platform, but what we didn't yet know is that by going far enough along the platform at most stations, we could cross the tracks to get where we were going. There was almost always an accessible route for the hand-carts and barrows which would work for me. We were comfortable in our own berths, this time, though, slept some and disembarked with no problem.

After a night at the Hotel Namaskar, in Delhi, we returned to the station to board the Shatabdi Express. The service was first class, and rather like being on an airplane. The attendants constantly brought us fruit juice, food, tea, newspapers and more tea.

We arrived in Dehra Dun shortly after lunch. Moti was waiting for us at the station. She had been a major in the Indian Army before she retired to work as a health educator and she was a great character, forthright and matter-of-fact. We took auto rickshaws to her house while she rode alongside on her motor scooter. Belinda and Moti struck up an immediate rapport. I was a little intimidated by her brusque manner but Moti took a great liking to Ross, who made several electrical repairs during our stay.

We hired a taxi to take us from Dehra Dun to Mussoorie. The road wound up and up, switchback upon switchback. "Yes, I have done this before!" I exclaimed in a few places; this particular turn and that outlook I knew. Logging had been extensive along the route, but in the distance were still the snow-covered Himalayas. As the preferred summer holiday spot for wealthy Indians who previously spent their vacations in now-troubled Kashmir, Mussoorie was full of hotels.

Our taxi driver let us off at the town library where we started up a steep hill. We had brought a rope with us and Belinda tied one end to her belt and the other to my chair. She pulled, and Ross and I pushed. We went on and on, up and up. I thought Belinda might give up, but we made it to the top, where we found a grand hotel that had previously been a palace. We had tea and lunch in the garden there, at 7,200 feet above sea level. We were just above the smog line and it was the first time we'd seen a really blue sky since coming to India. I imagined my very pregnant mother plodding along the streets of Mussoorie and through the bazaars and passionately knitting in her room at the guesthouse as she anticipated my birth. As we rode back down the hill from Mussoorie that evening in the taxi, I thought of the last ride my mother had made on that road: clutching Rosamond on her lap, anxiously watching me on the stretcher, thankful for the prayers that had gone up for me in Mussoorie from people in all sectors of society and from all denominations—Hindu, Sikh, Muslim, Christian. It was those prayers she was convinced had saved my life.

After a four-day stay we said our goodbyes to Moti and caught the Shatabdi Express back to Delhi. From there we planned to visit some of the famous sites of India, including the Taj Mahal.

We arranged for a driver to pick us up in Agra and take us to Jaipur. He stopped frequently along the way for a fresh supply of paan, the betel-nut concoction that so many Indians chew, particularly in the northern part of the country. Everywhere people walked were splots of red, looking like blood. Betel is said to have a mildly intoxicating effect, but we were told the mixtures could contain tobacco and sometimes even cocaine or opium, which accounts for paan's addictive quality. Our driver refused all our offers of fruit and biscuits, and ate nothing during the six-hour drive—only paan.

Ross and Belinda took turns in the unpopular front seat—unpopular because of Indian driving habits and our previous experience on the highways. After lunch at a roadside restaurant, nobody wanted the front seat. I perched on the edge of the back seat, with Ross lying on the seat behind me and Belinda lying on the floor at my feet. Our driver passed every vehicle we encountered, as drivers in India do, and each time he pulled out to pass, I would watch nervously and calculate whether he had time to complete the maneuver. In this way, I was behaving like my mother who was always a very nervous passenger. About fifteen minutes outside Jaipur, our driver pulled out to pass a lorry, and approaching in the oncoming lane was another lorry—one of the terrifying orange TATA vehicles. I knew by this time the lorries using these roads gave no quarter even to each other, let alone to a mere Ambassador taxi. Sure enough, nobody swerved, and BANG! We hit the lorry head on. Luckily, neither vehicle was going too fast.

The front of the taxi was smashed, the hood folded in half. I split my lip and broke the frame of my glasses, and I could soon feel that my ribs were either bruised or cracked. Belinda was asleep at the time, but we discovered later that she'd suffered a bit of a misplaced jaw. That evening at dinner, her back teeth didn't quite line up. However, the next day as she was eating there was a click and her jaw snapped back into place. Ross was completely unscathed. He got us out of the car and into some shade at the side of the road. The driver appeared to be completely fine. Ross got all our bags out, too, and moved them well away from the taxi as it was dripping petrol. When we had settled down a bit Ross went back to the scene of the accident, where by this time a large crowd had formed. Nobody had come over to see how we were and Ross allowed himself thirty seconds of shouting at the taxi driver and the lorry driver, gesticulating wildly. The two drivers looked sheepish as the eager crowd watched with great interest. In spite of not understanding English, I'm certain both drivers knew exactly what he was saying.

The three of us crossed to the other side of the highway to attempt to flag down a passing vehicle. After a short wait, an empty tourist mini-bus on its way to Jaipur airport stopped and took us the last eight kilometers of our journey. The bus dropped us off at a hotel called the Rajastani Palace, where we collapsed at a table in the lovely, quiet walled garden with marble sculptures of Hindu deities set into alcoves here and there. This hotel was definitely beyond our budget, Ross and I assumed, though Belinda pleaded for us to stay. Off she went to the office to inquire, and amazingly there were rooms available within our budget. Not only that—our room was also completely wheelchair accessible, including the width of the bathroom door, and there was plenty of hot water from a geezer, the on-demand electric hot water heaters found in many Indian bathrooms.

On the lane behind our hotel, three temporary wedding pavilions were being constructed. These structures, fashioned from bamboo and pole frames roped together and covered with brightly coloured fabric, were strung with many lights, carpeted and elaborately decorated. Sometimes weddings cost the bride's family a debt from which they would never recover. In the evening, we watched the families arrive. The children were all attired in new clothes, and a toy seller was taking advantage of the indulgence of their parents. There are no more beautifully or colourfully dressed women anywhere in the world than at an Indian wedding celebration, the vibrant oranges, greens, turquoises, royal blues, magentas, yellows and purples complimented by gold jewellery set with a myriad of coloured gems. One family invited us come into their pavilion and gave us a sort of hot coffee/chocolate drink, very sweet. A paan table had been set up with everyone, including the children, partaking.

The groom arrived on a white horse, wearing a red turban trimmed with tinsel which his mother spent much time arranging. The bride was led to the stage on which sat two throne-type chairs for the couple. Her transparent red chiffon sari, encrusted with floral sequin designs, was trimmed with a thick border of paisley made of the same iridescent white sequins. A garland of yellow and red marigolds encircled her neck. She kept her head bent as befit a Hindu bride. We caught an occasional glimpse of her nose ring from which hung a triangular ornament, made of pearl- and ruby-coloured stones set in gold, laid out in rows tapering to a gold pendant. This ornate nose-ring was attached to one of her elaborate earrings by a pearl and ruby chain. When she glanced up, we could see that the bindi between the bride's eyes was also pearl and ruby, and a delicate row of red and white dots in flower petal design was arched over each eyebrow. Her mehndi-covered hands were adorned with rings connected to pearl and ruby links that ended at her wrists, which were thick with eight inches of bangles. Around her neck hung a necklace heavy with rows and rows of pearl, ruby and gold in a motif patterned on the nose-ring and forehead pendant. The weight of her wedding apparel must have been enormous. Our landlady at the hotel described her own wedding day to us, and recalling how uncomfortable her nose ring had become as the day progressed.

The music from the three weddings was very loud, as is all of the music played through speakers in India. As Belinda said, "Indians don't love noise; they worship it!"

Constant car horns; popular and devotional music amplified to the point of distortion; people shouting, arguing, and singing; generator after generator in the shopping districts during the frequent power cuts; scooters, motorcycles, lorries, bells on bicycles and rickshaws: these were some of the sounds of India. No matter where we stayed, we'd hear a loud conversation beginning at 4:30 in the morning within earshot. Cars and vans made a multitude of sounds when backing up—"Santa Claus is Coming To Town," Christmas carols, "It's a Small World After All," the sound of a baby crying, and a mechanical voice that said, "This car is now backing up" over and over. My mother's India would have been a quieter place. Certainly in the towns and cities she would have heard shouting, singing, bicycle bells and calls to prayer, but at the bungalow a calm would have reigned, broken at times by the cry of peacocks or chanting or at a festive occasion, Molar's brass band. She sometimes chose to break the silence by playing Strauss waltzes or popular music on the phonograph.

From Jaipur, we travelled to Pushkar, also in Rajasthan, a lovely, little whitewashed town surrounding a lake. With its absence of vehicles, Pushkar was a welcome respite from noise and pollution. Cows, dogs, people and bicycles moved about at an unhurried pace, and families of strange long snouted, bristly pigs were everywhere.

The Rajasthani men wore huge turbans in red, yellow, bright magenta and orange. They are traditionally a warrior people, and their

Judy and her daughter Belinda in India.
(photo by Ross Hunt)

pride and honour showed clearly in their bearing. We took a ride into the desert with three men as our guides, Ross and I riding in a camel cart and Belinda on her own camel. After an hour and a half hour we came to the home of Raj, the owner of the camels. There were charpoys for us to sit on, and Raj's wife served us tea. She would not allow Ross and me to see her face, which she kept covered by her sari at all times. Raj said she wouldn't show her face to us in front of him, but she would show Belinda if she went to their kitchen, in a small outdoor courtyard. For Belinda she uncovered her face with no shyness and smiled, and Belinda came back and told us that she was pretty. As we rode back, through a spectacular desert sunset, Raj and his helpers were all singing a song that sounded familiar. After humming along for a while, I realized that it was Bob Marley's "Buffalo Soldier."

At the impressive ancient city of Amber Fort, Ross went exploring while Belinda and I stayed in the main courtyard to visit with the monkeys and elephants. We had passed many beautifully painted elephants on our way up to the Fort. As I said hello to one, she took my arm tightly in her trunk and gave it a small jerk. She could have flipped me into the air with one quick movement. Instead, she looked straight at me as if to say, "You just be aware of who I am!"

At the airport in Jaipur, I was surprised to see a washroom with the international wheelchair symbol on the door. There was a large wheeled scaffold in front it, so I went to look for assistance. Finally, Ross and Belinda and I decided to move the scaffolding ourselves. As we were doing so, someone came rushing up and said there was actually no washroom behind the door—it was just a façade. I made do in the regular ladies' toilet.

Wheelchair accessibility in India is by sheer fluke and good luck. Toilets were a constant challenge. In hotels with bathroom doorways that were too narrow, I partly folded my chair and roped it into that position. It was uncomfortable and awkward to sit on it that way, but it did allow me access. Ross got good at measuring with his feet when he was checking out a place. To pee on trains, I would discreetly position the appropriate part of my anatomy over a plastic container, with a shawl and Belinda or Ross providing a bit of concealment. Once the lid was back on the potty, one of my faithful travelling companions would take care of it. We worked out a different system for overnight train journeys. All of the trains we were on had both a western toilet and a squatter. Ross would go in first to clean the seat, and Belinda would piggyback me in and then out again. In hotels that had a squatter level with the floor, I could bring my chair close enough and hang my bottom over. If the squatter was on a raised platform, I would have to get out and sit on it. I worked by the "one elimination at a time" method.

Bombay (now Mumbai), the city where my parents had been married, was a rather arduous experience for us. We arrived at night and hoped to get an airport retiring room, since I was still suffering painful ribs from our car accident and had the flu. Although I begged, pleaded, lost my temper and told the official my father had lived in India for many years and would be ashamed to see how I was being treated, it was no go. We got on a bus headed for a hotel where rooms were advertised at 700 rupees. When we arrived, we discovered the room was 1100 rupees plus extra for a cot. Ross asked some taxi drivers about other hotels and two drivers got into a big shouting fight about who would take us. One driver even slapped the other!

In the end, the first hotel came down to 700 rupees for a dingy miserable room and brought in a lumpy mattress for Belinda. In the morning, she was covered in bed-bug bites. Ross and I had a few bites ourselves.

There is much poverty in Bombay, side by side with middle class living and wealth. Little shacks made from cardboard, tin and canvas stood all along the sidewalks, with families getting up, getting ready for school, and work, and kids shitting on the sidewalk. I was amazed at seeing people come out of these Bombay hovels and shacks dressed like any ordinary Indian citizens, the men in pressed dress trousers and shirts, school children in uniforms and neatly braided hair with ribbons. Bombay is home to some of the world's most expensive real estate, yet as many as 40% of the city's population lives in slums enduring constant run-ins with the authorities. Neighbourhoods like these are sometimes bulldozed to make way for other housing projects.

We travelled in southern India for several weeks. The beaches of Goa and Kovalum and the water tank in Varkala satisfied my swimmer daughter. We floated down the peaceful canals of Kerala, and walked through the lush parks of Bangalore. Kanyakumari, at the tip of India, was a thrill; the Bay of Bengal, the Indian Ocean and the Arabian Sea roll in from three different directions, and each can be seen distinctly.

12

travels south

EVERYONE TOLD US to go to Hampi. The strange land formations, temples and palaces of Hampi delighted us and at the Hubli rail station, we saw our first hijra, men who dress and behave as women. The hijra sub-culture is a very old one, both Islamic and Hindu in origin. Some are hermaphrodite, and a few have undergone castration. In the Hindu tradition hijras are looked down upon as an untouchable class. They turn up at weddings and at the birth of boy babies, much to the discomfort of the upper castes, to give their blessing by singing, dancing and performing religious ceremonies to bring good luck and fertility. If they are not given enough money, they will threaten to place a curse on someone or to lift their skirts and expose themselves. For the low castes, the arrival of the hijras is welcomed.

One evening in Hampi, as Belinda and I were leaving our room, a woman and a man approached a couple sitting in a neighbouring doorway. The man was playing a drum, and the woman was dressed in a red sari with much ornamentation and tinkling bells on her ankles. "You have come to see the temples and you don't want to see me, a temple dancer, dance?" she asked in a haughty voice. Belinda whispered into my ear, "That's a man!" We followed the hijra down some dark alleys and found her again at a restaurant. This time she was dancing with grace. A long well-oiled braid hung down her back and her full lips were painted scarlet. She had a lovely face with very fine features, and high cheekbones and arched brows over her kohl-rimmed eyes, though she displayed an expression of grumpy resignation: "I must do this again and again for these stupid people." We were fascinated and we gave her a well-deserved donation. Was the drummer her manager, her pimp, or her lover, or was she the one in charge of their business? I would love to have known their story. A group of children from the restaurant followed us as we left, and we asked one if she knew the dancer. She said she did. "Larka or larki?" we asked. Boy or girl? She said "Larka," boy, and all the children giggled.

We walked and walked in Hampi, sometimes seeing other tourists, sometimes seeing no one at all. Curious adolescents surrounded us hundreds of times a day, asking, "What is your name?" and "What is your country?" How to explain it? My country now is Canada, but the Indian spirit is at my core.

At an outdoor restaurant, I watched a bizarre entertainer put on a show a musical performance. He was playing two pipes through his nose and two pipes with his mouth. Meanwhile his assistant poured water into one of the pipes in his nose through a funnel. The water came out through one of the pipes in his mouth and into a plastic bottle. Indians have so many ingenious ways of making a living. From time to time in Hampi we would see the same group of three small children. One little girl was dressed as Sita, a Hindu goddess, a small boy was dressed as Hanuman, the monkey god, and another boy playing a drum accompanied them. The boys sang and the girl danced. I could imagine their parents dressing them up and sending them out to make a living from the tourists.

Three hundred kilometres south of Hampi is located the Mudumalai Forest Preserve. We were awoken at 6:00 AM with tea and coffee to begin our elephant ride. Seven elephants were being readied to carry passengers in a howdah, a cushioned seat with a railing around it that sits on the back of the elephant. Each elephant could carry four or five passengers plus the mahout, the elephant driver. There was a sturdy set of stairs constructed in the jungle clearing to climb up to reach the elephant's back. Belinda packed me up, and I got on easily. I was teary-eyed as we rode through the forest. At the company Christmas parties held each year for the village children at Bisunderpur, there was always a hired elephant to take us on rides.

Our guide pointed out a herd of spotted deer, a large deer called a sambar, peacocks and scratches on a tree that had been made by a panther. There was a population of about fifty tigers in the park, he told us, rarely seen until the dry season, when they come out of the deep forest for water. Wild elephants and wild boar roamed freely in the area, and we later saw two of each, on the other side of the river. On our way back to the lodge, we noticed four elephants being washed in the river by their keepers. The two smallest ones were playing in the water, one climbing on the other's back. The elephants being bathed were from a camp for sick, injured and orphaned elephants.

Later, Belinda and I headed off to see the sweetest little orphan elephant there, four months old. He let us touch him, and he investigated Belinda's feet with his little trunk. He kept very close to his mahout, hid his face against the man whenever he'd had enough of people and winding his trunk around his mahout's leg.

The monkeys in the forest preserve were a delight, especially the Bonnet Macaques. Belinda bought a bag of chips and fed them. They had old wrinkled little faces, and we decided one looked just like a neighbour at home. On our walks, Belinda entertained the village girls by making funny faces and doing funny walks until they were hysterical with laughter. The people who lived in the area were aboriginal tribal people, small and dark. The women wore a sarong wrapped over their breasts, sometimes with a shawl over that. They washed their clothing and bathed in the river near the lodge, and the local people took care of the elephants in the preserve. Every time we went down the road to the lodge, several children came forward to push my chair. Sadly, the people here faced a lot of discrimination. The manager at the lodge told us they were "primitive," and when we left Mudumalai we passed a building with a large sign that read "School for the Backward Classes." India tries to provide special education for tribal and other lower caste citizens, but I can't help feeling a school labeled that way, might further isolate the students.

Mysore is famous for its incense and the place really did have a lovely scent. The city didn't cater to western tourists much at all. We wanted some relief from the very spicy, south Indian food, and we decided on the Kwality Restaurant. My mother had frequented the Kwality Ice Cream Shop in Mussoorie; the shop figured in many of her accounts of hill station life, so the very name had a nostalgic ring. Ross ordered spaghetti that was burned on top and had a horrible taste. That's what happens when you try and get Italian food in Mysore.

Later in the day, while eating a fine dinner in the restaurant of a nearby hotel we discovered our favourite Indian menu quote: "Disposable vomit bags are available on request in case of need as a consideration to fellow diners."

The market in Mysore was partitioned off with a thick stone fence with narrow openings. "Sir, can we please borrow your stool?" said Ross to a shopkeeper. I sat on the borrowed stool while Ross and some boys lifted the wheelchair over the barriers. I squeezed between the stones and got back into my chair on the other side. It was an excellent market, filled with fruit, vegetables, flowers, incense and scented oils in every fragrance imaginable. Only now and again in Mysore would the regular Indian smells of sewer, cows and urine present themselves.

13

the train north

TO START OUR JOURNEY back from the south, we first caught a train for Bangalore, one hundred and fifty kilometres north of Mysore, and then two hundred and seventy-five kilometres east to Chennai, once known as Madras, on the Bay of Bengal. At the huge Chennai railway station, we caught a train for our two-day ride back north. We shared our berth with two nice young Indian men and an Italian by the name of Marino. Marino was the most unlikable person any of us had ever encountered. Ross chatted to him in Spanish, to which he reluctantly replied. He exuded a hateful energy. He may have been angry because I was in the bottom bunk, which was actually his, but it was no big deal for him to go one bunk up, while it would have been for me. In the morning, we gathered up our garbage and put it in a pile on the floor, ready to be put into a waste bin. Merino looked at the pile, looked at Ross, and then spat on the floor. He said, "You put garbage on the floor, I spit on the floor!" We explained that we didn't like to throw it out the window. Merino barked, "This is India!" So Ross threw our garbage out the window just like everybody else did. Marino continued to seethe with barely contained fury. He smoked constantly and barked at the chai and coffee sellers. He steadily smoked and farted and burped and spat (out the window, this time).

The long journey north was the most fun of all our train rides, but on the dirtiest train. The three of us read, wrote, ate, talked to the people we met and looked out the window. Meal orders taken at one stop would be ready at the next one. At one stop Ross almost missed the train and had to run very fast to jump back on.

The second night I moved to the opposite bottom bunk, so that Marino could have his proper spot back. He was up at 5:00 the next morning smoking, grumbling, farting and burping. He sat on the end of an Indian lady's berth and woke her up. When I heard him spit on the floor, I could no longer contain myself and I shouted at him, and he continued to spit on the floor repeatedly to provoke me. After a while, luckily, he grabbed his things and moved to another spot on the train. We were very glad to see him go. He'd been a little bit scary, and we wondered if he had a drug problem or perhaps a mental illness.

When the conductor checked our tickets that morning, an unticketed policeman was put off the train. He had been in a compartment with some older Buddhist ladies from Sri Lanka who were on a pilgrimage, and they later discovered he'd stolen a handbag from one of the women, containing all her money and her glasses. The conductor said there was no point in making a complaint to the police department, as the police would all stick together. The Indian police had a reputation for being very corrupt and the only time we would approach them was to ask for directions. Belinda and Ross and I each gave the poor lady 100 rupees. She was so grateful she came to our compartment, took our pictures and said she would pray for us.

14

Benares

Finally we had arrived at Varanasi, or as my parents always called it, Benares. My mother's first visit there was a shock. She was overwhelmed by the sick and dying pilgrims, the squalour, the smell of burning bodies at the ghats, the proximity of the beggars and the cows, and she escaped to the security of the car. She got accustomed to the sights and smells of Benares over time and grew to love the city—the bazaars selling their silks, brass, jewellery and trinkets, boat rides on the Ganges River, the worshipping bathers. I took to the place right away. The children in Benares were very street-wise and enterprising. One thirteen-year-old boy we met, Sanjay, had learned to speak several different languages from his dealings with the tourists who flocked to the holy Indian city.

Hindus come to Benares, the "eternal city," to die. Dying there means going immediately to heaven. Benares is the city of death, but also the city of life and rebirth. It has been a centre of learning and civilization for 2,000 years. The old part of the city worked its way down to the river in a series of narrow lanes between tall buildings. There was room in these alleys only for pedestrians, bicycles, cycle-rickshaws, the occasional scooter and the ever-present cows. The city bustled with crowds. Shops and offices and people's homes were all tucked in together. It was a fascinating, teeming place, with the happiest atmosphere of anyplace we had been. Even the beggars and lepers seemed full of radiance. Occasionally a procession of chanting men would pass by with drums and bells, carrying above their heads a body on a bamboo stretcher wrapped in a saffron or white cloth.

One morning we rented a boat to take us out on the river to watch the sun rise. From there, we could see the ghats, a series of stone steps leading to the water where people come to immerse themselves, pray, and bathe. There are over 100 ghats, one of the most famous being Manikarnika, the burning ghat. A caste of untouchables called Doms do the burning of corpses there. They are a traditional group who has always taken care of the cremation grounds and ghats, and it spite of being untouchables, they have a great deal of power and respect in the community. The head Dom is called the 'Raja Dom,' or 'King'.

While we were out in the boat, Belinda filled her empty water bottle with Ganges River water to bring home for a souvenir. Ross encouraged her to try to get ashes and sediment in it. After we returned to shore and were walking along to a restaurant, Ross realized all of a sudden, that he had drunk a good portion of the Ganga water from the bottle. He was horrified and close to panicking. Belinda and I stayed and ate our breakfast while Ross and Kimberly, a woman we had met on the train, went to find a doctor. They eventually found one, and Ross was given anti-viral and anti-bacterial drugs to combat anything he might have picked up from the water. We assured him that now he was especially holy.

I investigated some silk shops with Kimberly. Our ride to the shops was my first time in a cycle-rickshaw. It was a bit bumpy, but so nice and quiet. We moved with the flow of bicycles, cycle-carts, barrows and handcarts, some piled with goods to extreme heights. An occasional horse-drawn cart or bullock-cart plodded by.

In the evening, we enjoyed a north Indian meal of thick, rich chick-pea dahl, subji and chappatis. It was wonderful to be in the north of India again. I was back my neighbourhood, back with the cunning, clever and witty people I felt so comfortable with. The hustle and bustle, noise and apparent confusion all felt like home.

Following our meal, we walked down to the Dasaswamedh ghat, one of the largest and most central of the ghats. Legend tells that ten horses were once sacrificed there by Lord Brahma to allow Lord Shiva to return from a period of banishment. Belinda packed me down the stairs and the others again took the chair. We were offered a good price for a boat ride to Manikarnika ghat, so we all piled in. I was full of awe and reverence to be so close to the cremation site, but it was also dramatic to be able to see burning bodies. Three were in the last stages of burning. One was lit as we watched and another was brought down to the sacred water for a final immersion before cremation. Huge piles of wood were ready at hand. The government had built electric crematoriums in Benares and other parts of India, but even though the cost is less than a traditional wood-fired cremation, the newer method was not very popular and mostly used for the dead who have no families. The procuring of firewood for cremations causes immense environmental damage in India.

Kimberly took out her camera as we approached the burning ghat. I told her it was forbidden to photograph there, and I'm sure she must have read that in her travel guide, but she made the foolish mistake of snapping a picture, flash and all. Our boatman said, "Now the watchman will come and fine you." Instead of continuing on with the boat ride, he lingered near the shore, and sure enough down came the watchmen. Two of them climbed aboard the boat. They were angry. "You must give us 500 rupees!" they demanded of Kimberly. "If you don't pay the fine we must take you to the office." She had no cash with her, so I lent her the money. Our boatman went ashore for a few minutes with the watchmen and was given, I suspect, his percentage. At the end of the ride, he asked for a tip. "I think you have already received your tip, Mr. Boatman," we said. He didn't ask again. Later, Belinda's street-wise friend Sanjay told us there was no watchmen's office. It was disrespectful of Kimberly to take a photo, knowing the taboo, but she was rather an impulsive young woman.

Everywhere we went in India my wheelchair and its workings were of enormous interest to the men and boys. After much studying and pointing, someone would always say, "Ahh, brraake, acha." We always attracted a crowd. Ross loved to demonstrate the brakes on my chair and the quick-release wheels, which often had to be removed to fit into rickshaws.

In Benares we stayed at the Old Yogi Lodge. (The city also had the Yogi Lodge, the Jogi Lodge, the New Yogi Lodge, the Gold Yogi Lodge and more.) The Old Yogi Lodge was down a narrow alley off Luxa Road. It was a funky four-storey building with a central common area used for meals and games and general hanging out. Ross and I had a very basic room on the ground floor, with a squatter toilet and a shower that dribbled occasional hot water. Belinda's room was on one of the upper floors. But the family atmosphere and the lodge's proximity to the ghats were perfect for us. It was run by a family of dude-wallahs, people in the dairy caste, and the mother made the best yoghurt we had ever tasted. Her sons, Bacha and Babu ran the hotel business.

One afternoon Belinda and I headed down to the Dasaswamedh ghat, a perfect place to watch the crowds. Who should we see as we strolled along, but Marino, our offensive Italian train companion! He had a very pleasant look on his face and he smiled and inclined his head when we said hello. It was difficult to imagine that he was the same person. We may have been right about him needing his fix in Benares.

15

Goodbye to Mirzapur

LOUD MUSIC PLAYED constantly in the bazaars of northern India, generally songs from Hindi Bollywood movies. There was one song we heard everywhere. In the streets and in the laneways, children would be singing it as well. "Pardesi, pardesi, jana nahine. Pardesi, pardesi, jana nahine…" Ross went into a tape shop, hummed a little of the tune and asked if they knew what it was. It was the hit song from the current hit movie, *Raja Hindustani* they said. We were back in Mirzapur by now, and one day when we went into town with Kusum we noticed that *Raja Hindustani* was playing at the town cinema. Belinda decided to do errands with Kusum while Ross and I went to the movie. Since we were early, we spent some time in a small tidy park full of hollyhocks, roses, poppies and marigolds. Stone busts of Independence freedom fighters lined the walkway.

We wandered through town on our way to the theatre. This was the place where I had been pushed in my pram as a baby and walked hand in hand with my adoring mother as a small child. I thought about the many changes my mother would have noticed. In her time, widows wore white, and unless it was a festive occasion, peasant women and girls were clad in colourless saris made of unbleached cotton. Now, thanks to inexpensive polyester, all women, regardless of caste, wore saris and salwar kameez in bright rainbow shades. A parade of groups were marching, drumming, chanting and dancing in the streets to promote student elections at the local college. Everyone seemed to be having a jolly time, but many police stood by in case things got out of hand.

We thoroughly enjoyed the film, even though we couldn't always tell what was going on. There was plenty of comedy and lots of dancing and singing and drama, plus we got to hear our favourite song, 'Pardesi', over and over. Indian movies are long, over three hours, and during the intermission snack sellers roamed about selling goodies to the audience.

Kusum and Geoffrey's driver, Nuncoo, was waiting for us when the movie was over. He drove us to the house of some friends of Kusum's, where she and Belinda were already visiting. The beautiful old bungalow was on the banks of the Ganges, land that was washing away so rapidly during each monsoon that one day the house would be no more. Kusum's friend and her daughter-in-law served us tea and sandwiches and at Kusum's request I sang "Love Song for the Women in My Life," a song I had written for International Women's Day some years before. It was fitting for the company we were in.

We were invited to Bisunderpur with a number of other guests to have dinner with Edward Oakley, who worked for the carpet company Obeetee. Edward was the son of Wilfred and Elaine Oakley, old friends of my parents. First we had drinks at the Mirzapur Club that was directly across the road from Edward's bungalow. Edward made a grand late entrance. He was a marvellously eccentric character who seemed to enjoy talking nonsense and confusing people. The large bungalow where he entertains guests sat across the street from our family bungalow, and I had visited there with my mother many times as a child.

Edward's dining room was enormous. The long table was set elaborately, with many different knives, forks and spoons, water glasses, and glasses for red wine and glasses for white. A fresh plate was produced for every course. We started with soup, then followed by turkey, roast potatoes, Brussels sprouts, parsnips, sausages, bacon and gravy, with trifle for dessert. Five servants offered the dishes to each dinner guest in turn. Edward held forth at the head of the table. He had been born in India, but he and I had never met, since he and his sister had been sent away to England to school by the time I was born. Edward had built up a spectacular estate and his servants obviously held him in high regard, as he did them. Ross and Belinda and I were mesmerized by it all.

Finally it was time to leave Raipuri. We packed up our things and bid a sad, fond farewell to the staff: Krishna, Dilari, Rita, Ram Lal, the drivers, the mali and the chowkidar. We exchanged hugs and goodbyes and thank-yous with Geoffrey, then set off in the Ambassador with Kusum, our driver, and Poonu, down the famous Grand Trunk Road to Benares.

16

leaving india

WHILE WE WERE in Benares, Belinda wanted me to come with her to visit her friend Sanjay. We made our way through a maze of laneways, some so narrow that once we had to ask a man to move his parked scooter so my chair could get by. Sanjay lived with his aunt and uncle, sister and cousin in one tiny room. A black and white TV played non-stop on a high shelf in the corner of the room, except for two short periods when the power went out during our visit—a frequent Indian occurrence. The room was one of several off the narrow alley, each home to a family. Food was prepared on a cooker just outside the doorway. Sanjay's sister made chai for us, and his uncle and I talked. He was very apologetic about his home, but I assured him it was an honour to experience his hospitality.

We were all sad at the prospect of leaving India. One morning I cried on Ross's shoulder. The next day I came into our room and Ross was crying. "I just saw a cow walk by the window," he said, and he knew that soon that would be happening no more. Belinda spent entire days playing with the neighbourhood kids in the lane outside the Old Yogi Lodge. They loved her also. Babu, the hotel manager, said to me, "Belinda is famous!"

"Mom, let's go to Dasaswamedh again," Belinda said one morning. "It will be our last time." She and I took a rickshaw to the ghats and she bumped me down the steps to the river's edge. It was my fourth time on the Ganges, and Belinda's seventh. She worked hard to pull me and my chair back up the stairs, refusing all help from bystanders. On the way we stopped to buy a few bits and pieces: a neem twig for cleaning teeth, some stickers and a painted plastic Hanuman, the monkey god, Belinda's favourite Hindu deity. Kusum had told us that Hanuman stood for strength and celibacy.

We filled two tin trunks with the treasures we had accumulated during our travels. On our last day in Benares, Belinda stayed at the hotel to play with her friends while Ross and I took one more jaunt to the bazaar. The next morning, we bid farewell to the excellent cook, Moti Lal, the family who owned the hotel, and the neighbourhood kids and their mothers. We needed three rickshaws to take us and all our bags and trunks to the train station. I found a place to write in my journal while Ross took a seat on a nearby bench joining two Muslim women in black burkas, and two sari-clad women with their children.

Not wanting to jam on with the hordes of travellers, we had decided to wait until things settled down. On all of our railway journeys, we had boarded, then waited a considerable time before the train left the station. This time, a man nearby looked at us with a rather worried expression and said, "I think you'd better get on the train."

There we were with our nine pieces of luggage, including the two large tin trunks, plus me and the chair, all to be loaded quickly onto the train. Ross and Belinda carried the trunks on first and found our seat. Belinda came running back for me. She set me down in the first available spot, and then ran back to the platform for the rest of our bags. As I sat there waiting, the train began to move. Slowly at first, and then faster and faster. I panicked, as I haven't yet seen the other two. Should I pull the stopping chain? I looked wildly for it, but it was out of my reach. Should I ask someone else to pull it? I tried to visualize how I would manage arriving in Delhi without my travelling companions or my wheelchair. My mind was racing, my heart pounding. Then a fellow passenger who could see the platform told me it was all right; Belinda and Ross had got on. I peered down the aisle, and there they were. I was weak with relief. They had run for the train, thrown on the bags and chair and Ross had to, with great force, push Belinda into the crowd of Indians who were standing in the doorway watching the proceedings. He swung on behind her, all in the nick of time.

India was full of surprises, as is life. Just when you think you have things figured out, you can be tricked. Travelling in India was a test and a challenge. The gods in India are numerous as are the methods of worship, but every Indian is a believer. Every Indian is filled with spirit and little prayer ceremonies, little pujas, happen everywhere.

I lay awake in my bunk for a long time, and after finally dropping off to sleep was woken by the chai wallah and his loud, rasping sing-song, "Chai, chai, gharam chai! Gharam chai!" It was 4:20 AM. At 8:15, we arrived in Delhi. We hired porters to carry our luggage to the taxi stand and took a cab to the YWCA Blue Triangle Family Hostel on Ashoka Road.

We had the afternoon to fill before it was time to leave for the airport. The three of us talked about the things we would miss on leaving India. We wouldn't miss the smells of urine or sewers or garbage. We wouldn't miss the choking pollution in the large cities like Jaipur and Delhi. But we would miss the smells of incense at every turn. We would miss the aromas and flavours of the food, spicy and savoury. We would miss the faces of the children and the ready smiles of people who could become your best friend in a moment. We would miss the geometrically piled heaps of fruit and vegetables in the bazaars, the bright colours of the women's clothing, the exotic jewellery and the wonderful fabrics. We would miss the docile friendly cows in the streets and alleys. We would miss the old, old feeling of some of the places we'd visited, and we would especially miss Benares, the ancient city we'd grown to love so well.

17

the memsahib

WHILE WE WERE flying backwards through time on our return to Vancouver, my mother woke in the night. Her heart was racing; her breath came in short gasps. She called a taxi to take her to the emergency ward at Lions Gate Hospital. There she was hooked up to monitors, questioned, poked and prodded and found to be in perfect health, except for a slight rise in blood pressure. That was not out of the ordinary for her. I believe she was having a panic attack, fearing that our plane would crash, fearing that she would never see me again. All the terrors she had experienced on flying herself no doubt flashed across the film screen of her mind: a ball of fire, twisted wreckage, bodies falling from the sky.

At the time we left for our journey to India, my mother was still adjusting to being a widow. She was excited for me, although she must have been quite worried. She had burst into tears of relief when I called her from Geoffrey and Kusum's house to let her know we'd arrived.

After my father's death, my mother had begun to lose interest in the things that normally filled her time. Her autumn and winter production of beautiful hand-spun, hand-dyed and hand-knitted sweaters ceased. She was no longer interested in food, except for cookies and ice-cream. The individual servings of soups, curries and stews Rosamond stashed in my mother's freezer remained untouched. And her short-term memory became noticeably deficient. My father had been her touchstone, her entertainment, her security and her link to the world outside. None of us saw her weep when he died. She put on a brave British front. But she did admit to missing him dreadfully. On one of her trips to visit me, it became clear that my mother was dependent on alcohol. She started to drink wine at ten in the morning.

Things began to unravel as my mother's dementia progressed. Once when Belinda and I visited she was sporting two black eyes. She had forgotten how she got them, but a neighbour told us she had fallen and hit her head in the bathroom at a strata party.

Before my father's death, my parents had had a lawyer draw up legal documents giving power of attorney to their three daughters. It was a wise move and a blessing, as Rosamond and I were able to take over my mother's affairs. Belinda, who had a special relationship with her Alla, as she called my mother, moved in to take care of her. We hoped that with regular meals, vitamins, company and sobriety, my mother's memory might improve. But her dementia progressed and some days she refused to believe Belinda was her granddaughter.

I came to stay with the two of them regularly. She sometimes seemed to see me as someone extra special and exceptional. She would tell Belinda how much she admired me and how amazing she thought I was. She often told her about the number of people that had prayed for me when I was in the hospital in Mussoorie. That experience had marked her. One evening she called me in to see a TV program about experimental electrical implants used in people with spinal chord injuries to stimulate motor nerves or muscles. "Judy, come and look. Perhaps they can do that to you. Perhaps you can walk again!" After a year of Belinda and Alla being roommates, my mother broke her hip. It became clear she couldn't come back to her apartment and would have to stay in extended care.

My mother's loss of memory has brought her peace, I think. She had so many worries, so much anxiety that she tried to keep strictly under control. It must be a comfort to let others take control. Just as the Bisunderpur bungalow has decayed, the events and circumstances of my mother's life have caused the walls of her mind to collapse, confusing the layers of time and memory. Stories surface that seem to come from wisps of her childhood and her early motherhood. "Where's that baby? Where's that baby I just had sitting on my lap?"

My mother is at home where she lives now. She always greets me warmly. "Oh, Judy, how lovely it is to see you!" If any residents or staff are nearby, she says proudly "This is my eldest daughter, Judy. She was born in India. You were born in India, weren't you?" The staff adores her. My mother's impeccable social skills have not abandoned her, nor has her wicked sense of humour. Troubled residents seem to gravitate to her and she is patient with those who cannot communicate clearly, at least to their faces. During one of my visits, an unintelligible conversation with another woman went on and on. When the woman finally turned in her wheelchair and left, Mom made a face to her retreating back, stuck out her tongue, and said, "Silly old fool!" She gave me a big grin.

epilogue

In 2007 after a space of eleven years, and after missing India every winter, Ross and I made a second trip back, spending most of our time in the Mirzapur district. While staying as the guests of Edward, at the old Oakley bungalow in Bisunderpur, across the road from the home where I had spent my first years, I was drawn back to our family's old home.

On a mid-December early afternoon, the sun filtering through the ever-present haze of the Indian sky, I set off down Edward's drive, past the potted chrysanthemums and manicured gardens, under the grapefruit trees and flowering mango trees, and through the gate to the road. I shared the road with bicycles, cycle rickshaws, pony drawn ekkas and the occasional motorcycle. Brick walls of varying heights stood behind the neem and mango trees on either side of the route.

When I came to the chained wrought-iron gate of the old E. Hill & Company bungalow, I looked through the bars. I could see four chowkidars in front of the house, one doing his morning wash. They stared curiously at me, and one came towards the gate carrying a round clay water pot. He unlocked a small door in the gate, leaving it open as he went to fetch water. I gestured to ask, "May I go in?" His half head wag and the open gate indicated that I could.

As I entered the grounds, I stopped on the path to look round. On either side of me the jungle trees were over-grown with thick hanging vines and surrounded by dense undergrowth. I began to cry.

Ahead was the bungalow. On rope strung between two trees, blankets and a lungi had been left to dry in the sun. I tried to converse with the young chowkidar who came up the path. "Mera ghar…baccha, ek, do, tin, char. Mera mammie, mera pita." My home…child, one, two, three, four. My mummy, my father, I offered, wiping my eyes and sniffing. The lad replied in rapid Hindi, and any words I might have recognized vanished. "Apka nam kya hai?" I asked his name—the one question I can always remember.

As I approached the house, I could see the three men preparing their afternoon meal. On a low charpoy sat a stainless steel tali tray with a huge mound of rice in the centre. There were remnants of a bonfire on the ground; it got cold at night this time of year. As I reached the bottom of the three stairs up to the verandah, I looked beyond into the house. I looked past the huge beams that had fallen from the roof, the piles of bricks and the thick leaf mold, to the opposite wall. There stood the fireplace of my childhood, now chipped and stained by monsoon rains. The bungalow was open to the sky. The chowkidars had created a small household for themselves under the verandah roof. Under one charpoy were a pair of polished black boots.

The back of the bungalow was a ruin, blackened and crumbling. I turned to look at the river. The wind made a steady whoosh as I took in the sound and the feel of it on my face. Crows cawed their standard caws, an unknown bird trilled, and the Seven Sisters birds chattered and squawked in their clusters as they moved from tree to tree. Beneath the bird sounds came the occasional bawl of a cow.

I moved to the edge of the riverbank, the Holy Mother Ganga below me. Four boats were on the grey-blue water, one with a rippling ochre sail. Twenty or thirty more were tied up below, and I could hear the chatter of children playing among them. Each year the bank had moved closer to the bungalow, over what was once the manicured lawn, eaten steadily by monsoons. A large acacia tree perched on the crumbling cliff-side would not last the next one. A small butterfly, peacock-blue, black and dusty brown, flitted by.

India will continue to call me. In the future, I may get there only through stories, or films, or food, but in my dreams, I will keep going back.

Glossary of Terms

Annas: a coin that is a small fraction of a rupee, no longer in use
Ayah: Indian nanny
Baksheesh: tip, bonus, charitable gift or in some cases a bribe
Barrhaee: carpenter
Bidi: hand-rolled cigarette
Burka: an outer garment that completely covers the body worn by some Muslim women
Burrah: big
Chai: Indian tea made with spices, milk and sugar
Charpoy: low cot made from a wooden frame strung with woven rope
Chowkidar: caretaker or watchman
Dahl: cooked lentils, an important source of protein
Dhobi: man or woman who does the laundry
Dhoti: a piece of fabric draped as a loincloth worn by some Indian men
Dirzi: tailor
Ekka: small pony cart
Ganga: Ganges River
Gharam: hot
Ghat: series of steps leading down to a river
Jaldi: hurry
Lathi: a cane, often carried by police
Lungi: wrap-around sarong garment worn by some Indian men, very common in southern India
Mali: gardener
Namaste: Hindu greeting, raised palms together
Pani: water
Papadums: large deep fried lentil chips
Pi dog: stray dogs found everywhere in India
Punkah: fan
Salwar kameez: loose, drawstring trousers with long tunic shirt
Sari: long piece of light fabric draped into a graceful garment worn by women in all
Tali: large stainless tray with indentations to hold servings of different curries, rice and chutneys
Topi: hat or cap, particularly a pith helmet
Tuc-tuc: three-wheeled auto-rickshaw used as a taxi
Wallah: a person connected with a particular thing or function

Acknowledgements

We want to thank the many people who have been helpful in the creation this book. Of course, some of those who were instrumental in assisting my mother with her manuscript may go unnamed, as my mother cannot tell me, but our gratitude goes out to them. We regret any omissions that might have occurred in the following list:

Gladys & Will Hargreaves, Meryl Chamberlain, Michael Norbury, Rosamond Bremner, Natalie & David Logan, Lyn Guy, Rosamond Norbury, Amanda Craig, Eliza Norbury Murbach, Belinda Norbury Murbach, Ben Murbach, Douglas Newby, Ross Hunt, Andrea, Doug & Steve Saba, Katherine Collins, Elaine Harvey, Sheila Munro, Geoffrey & Kusum Seager, Edward Oakley, Amrit Kocher & Family, Margaret Cadwaladr, Barbara Pulling, Janet Taylor, and John McKercher.

Photo Credits

Unless otherwise noted, all photographs are from the Norbury family collection. Colour photographs on front and back cover by Rosamond Norbury. We believe the photograph by R. H. Marlow is now in the public domain.

Also by Madrona Books

Speed's War

A Canadian Soldier's Memoir
of World War II

by George A. Reid

ISBN 0-9730096-2-0
$16.95 plus shipping/handling
(add GST in Canada)

In Veronica's Garden

The Social History of the
Milner Gardens and Woodland

by Margaret Cadwaladr

ISBN 0-9730096-1-6
$34.95 plus shipping/handling
(add GST in Canada)

Phone: 1-800-866-5504
Fax: 250-897-3286
E-mail: madronabooks@shaw.ca
www.madronabooks.com